LITURGY OF THE ANCIENT AND ACCEPTED SCOTTISH RITE OF FREEMASONRY,

[Annotated and Illustrated]

FOR THE SOUTHERN JURISDICTION OF THE UNITED STATES.

PART I.

I. To III.

By

Albert Pike

ISBN: 9781983292279

About the Bonificio Masonic Library

The Bonificio Masonic Library is an attempt to create the largest and most complete e-book library in Masonry, all funds earned from the purchase of our Kindle version books goes into the purchase, and transcription of further books so that Freemasons all over the world will have access to the necessary educational materials to develop and gain further light from Freemasonry, its symbols, history, and its meaning.

The Bonificio Masonic Library, has over 5500 books, which it is in the process of making available to every Mason, in an easy to read, and understandable format, so that you Brother, can possess all the light and knowledge available at your fingertips whenever and wherever the mood for some further light in Masonry strikes your mood.

In today's day and age, further light into the history, origins, meanings, and symbolism of our fraternity are more important than ever, and ready accessibility to the information at hand has a need for further dissemination to our Brethren where ever they may be dispersed.

So thank you for supporting us Brother's and friends of Freemasonry, and I hope you enjoy this book.

Visit our website to see all available titles:

http://thegrid.ai/bonificio-masonic-library/

Join us on Facebook:

https://www.facebook.com/groups/1515841082054855/

About the Book:

Albert Pike, 33, Sovereign Grand Commander (1859-91)

The Liturgy is the "manual" or "monitor" of the Scottish Rite Degrees of Freemasonry.

Each chapter of this book includes a depiction of the Degree's regalia, as well as a description of the Lodge, Chapter or Council, with its furniture, decorations, the officers, titles, etc., needed to confer the Scottish Rite Degrees.

This volume covers the rituals and symbolism of the first three Degrees (EA - FC), which comprise the Blue House. It includes extracts from the rituals and ceremonies, as well as the lectures for the Degrees, and an explanation in full of the symbolism on display for the newly made and longtime Mason alike.

LITURGY

OF THE

ANCIENT AND ACCEPTED SCOTTISH RITE

OF

FREEMASONRY,

FOR THE SOUTHERN JURISDICTION OF THE UNITED STATES.

PART I.

I. to III.

By: Albert Pike

Χαίρειν ων εάδαζ τάζ Τιμάζ τάζ των πολλων ανθρώπων, την 'ΑΛΗ' ΘΕΙΑΝ όχοπών, πειράοομαι τώ ύντι ώζ άν δύνωμαι βέλτιότοζ ων χαί ζην, χαί έπιδάν άποθνήόχω, άποΘνήχειν.

Wherefore bidding Farewell to the Honors of the Multitude, and having my eye upon Truth, I will endeavor, as far as I am able, to Live in the best manner I can, and when I Die, to Die so.—PLATO.

IN THE SUPREME COUNCIL
FOR THE SOUTHERN JURISDICTION OF THE UNITED STATES,

8th day of אייר, A∴ M∴ 5626.

"RESOLVED, That the Sovereign Grand Commander be requested to prepare a Manual for the various Degrees in the Ancient and Accepted Rite; and that the same, together with a work already prepared by him on the Morals and Dogma of the Rite, be published under his direction, at the expense of and under the sanction of this Supreme Council."

PROCLAMATION.	10
THE PORCH AND THE MIDDLE CHAMBER.	11
THE BOOK OF THE LODGE.	11
PROŒMIUM.	12
THE BLUE DEGREES.	17
MASONRY.	18
DEFINITION AND OBJECTS OF, ETC.	18
THE LODGE, IT'S OFFICERS, DECORATIONS, ETC.	19
VISITORS AND HONORS.	25
THE PROPOSING AND ELECTING OF MEMBERS.	26
REGULATIONS.	28
APARTMENTS CONNECTED WITH THE LODGE.	29
ORDER OF BUSINESS.	30
MISCELLANEOUS.	30
First Degree	34
I.	36
APPRENTICE.	36
OPENING.	36
INTRODUCTION OF VISITORS.	37
RECEPTION.	38
ORISONS.	43
PRAYER.	43
A.	50
THE AIR.	51
THE WATER.	53
אור.	58
העלמים.	60
ADDRESS OF THE ORATOR.	70

ADDRESS TO VISITORS.	70
ANOTHER.	70
THE FUGITIVE LEAVES.	71
PRAYER.	71
TABLE- OR BANQUET- LODGE.	72
ARRANGEMENT OF THE LODGE.	72
FIRST HEALTH.	72
SECOND HEALTH.	73
THIRD HEALTH.	73
FOURTH HEALTH.	73
FIFTH HEALTH.	73
SIXTH HEALTH.	74
SEVENTH HEALTH.	74
EIGHTH HEALTH.	74
NINTH HEALTH.	74
TENTH HEALTH.	74
LAST HEALTH.	75
PARTING SONG OF MASONS.	75
CLOSING- SONG.	76
𝕾econd 𝕯egree	78
II.	79
FELLOW-CRAFT—COMPAGNON.	79
TO OPEN.	80
PRELIMINARIES OF RECEPTION.	80
RECEPTION.	81
EXAMINATION.	82
MUSIC.	83
MUSIC.	85
MUSIC.	87

MUSIC.	89
MUSIC.	95
הנדרים.	97
MUSIC.	98
XII.	99

THIRD DEGREE 108

III.	109
MASTER.—MAITRE MAÇON	109
ESSENTIAL INTRODUCTION.	109
THE MIDDLE CHAMBER.	110
TITLES.	111
CLOTHING.	111
OPENING.	111
PRAYER.	111
ODE.	111
III.	112
PRELIMINARIES OF RECEPTION.	112
RECEPTION.	113
PREPARATION OF THE CANDIDATE.	113
MUSIC.	119
MUSIC.	124
PRAYER.	129
MUSIC.	130
X∴ LEGEND AND DRAMA.	130
EVENING HYMN OF THE WORKMEN.	132
MUSIC.	136
PRAYER.	137
MUSIC.	138
FUNERAL CHANT AND HYMN.	138

FINAL INSTRUCTION	142
APPENDIX	150
OFFICES OF CONSECRATION.	151
PRELIMINARY DIRECTIONS.	151
THE CHAIRMAN.	152
MUSIC.	152
CHAUNT.	153
ODE.	155
CHAUNT.	156
Jubilate Deo.	156
CHAUNT.	157
CHAUNT.	157
Laudate Dominum.	157
CHAUNT.	158
Confitemini Domino.	158
PRAYER	159
SONG	159

PROCLAMATION.

The Liturgy, Monitor, or Manual, of the Ancient and Accepted Scottish Rite of Freemasonry, as that Rite is practiced in the Southern Jurisdiction of the United States (of which Liturgy the pages that follow constitute the First Part), has been prepared by the Sovereign Grand Commander, in pursuance of the Resolution on a preceding page, and accords with the Ritual of the Rite approved by the Supreme Council.

It is hoped that it may not prove entirely unworthy of the acceptance and consideration of the Craft, and that it may prove useful to the initiated.

Nothing whatever, contained in this Liturgy, or in the Rituals of the Degrees of the Rite, has been copied or borrowed from any other modern Liturgy, Monitor, Manual, or Ritual; and whatever is the same in the Liturgies and Rituals, and Books of Ceremonies or Offices, of the Southern Jurisdiction, and in the Book of the Ancient and Accepted Rite, by Bro∴ Charles T. McClenachan, or in any Ritual, or Book of Ceremonial, of the Northern Jurisdiction, has been borrowed and copied from our Rituals and Books of Ceremonies.

The Author and Compiler has no pecuniary interest in these or in any works published for use in the Southern Jurisdiction ; all have been published by and for the benefit of the Supreme Council, for which the copyrights have been secured, and to which they have been assigned.

THE PORCH AND THE MIDDLE CHAMBER.

THE BOOK OF THE LODGE.

PROŒMIUM.

A Rite[1] of Freemasonry, is a scale or series of Degrees, more or less in number, following each other in regular order, and worked as a System, under one Governing Body.

Many Rites have been and are worked; the principal of which, at the present day, are what are commonly known as the English or York Rite; the Ancient and Accepted Scottish Rite; and the Rit Moderne or French Rite. Of other Rites, now or heretofore used, we may name those of Fessler, of Schroder of Hamburg, of Strict Observance, and of Swedenborg, and that of Perfection or of Heredom.

The three Blue Degrees, Apprentice, Fellow-Craft or Companion, and Master, belong to and form a part of all the principal Rites. The Rite of Perfection commenced with them, and so do the Ancient and Accepted Scottish Rite, and the Rit Moderne.

There, are great variances between the English work and that of the United States, in the Degrees of the York or English Rite: and the work of those Degrees is quite different in the York and the Ancient and Accepted Scottish Rite; while the work of the latter and that of the Rit Moderne in the same Degree, in the main, agree.

The Rite of Perfection, in twenty-five Degrees, the 25th being the Sublime Prince of the Royal Secret, was arranged and worked on the Continent of Europe, or at least in France, prior to the year 1762. The Ancient and Accepted Scottish Rite was formed by the intercalation of seven Degrees in the Rite of Perfection, and some other slight changes, made toward the end of the 18th century.

---

[1] Ritus (Lat.), the form and manner of religious observances, a religious usage or ceremony. Graeco ritu sacra non Romano facere. Qvo haec priva- Um et pvblice modo ritvqcoe fiant, disconto ignari a pvblicis sacerdotibvs. — Cicero, de Legib. Morem ritusque sacrorum adjiciam.—Virgil. Ex patriis ritibvs optvma colvnto.—Cicero, Legib. Also, a custom, usage, manner, mode, way. Ritus, mos vel consuetudo. Cognosse Sabinae Gentis ritus.

The root of the word is the Sanskrit and Ancient Aryan verb ऋ ri, "to go, to rise," whence riti, 'way,' rita, "rising, regularity, truth,' and ritu, 'order, the right time, for sacrificing, sacrifice, ceremonial.' The Latin Orior, 'to rise/ oriens, 'east/ are from this root.

The Rit Moderne, established by the Grand Orient of France in 1786, consists of Seven Degrees, the three first being the Blue Degrees, and the others, Elu, Ecossais ∴Chevalier d'Orient and Chevalier Rose-Croix, which was the 18th of the Rite of Perfection, and is the 18th of the Ancient and Accepted Scottish Rite. The Supreme Bodies of this Rite are called Grand Chapters General.

The Ancient and Accepted Scottish Rite, consisting of thirty-three Degrees, of which the first three are the Blue Degrees, is governed and administered by bodies of the 33d Degree, called Supreme Councils. Of these, the oldest existing one in the world is that for the Southern Jurisdiction of the United States, whose See is at Charleston. It was established on the 31st of May, 1801; and from it all other Supreme Councils now existing have, mediately or immediately, originated. In France there are two, the Grand Orient of France having, about 1815, established one within itself, when the members of the Supreme Council for France, of which the Arch-Chancellor Cambaceres was Sov∴ Grand Commander, had been dispersed upon the re- turn of the Bourbons.

The Supreme Council for the Northern Jurisdiction of the United States was established at New York, by the Supreme Council of the United States at Charleston, in 1813, and was afterward removed to Boston.

The Supreme Council for France and its dependencies was established by the Comte Alexandre Auguste de Grasse, Founder of the Supreme Council at Charleston, and of that for the Windward and Leeward French West Indian Islands, in Santo Domingo, in 1802. He created the Supreme Council of France in 1804, and afterward revived that of America [the West Indies] about 1815, which afterward united with the Supreme Council for France.

The Supreme Council of Belgium was established in 1817, by authority of the Supreme Council of France; that of Ireland, in 1826, by the Supreme Council for the Southern Jurisdiction of the United States; that for Scotland, in 1846, by the Supreme Council of France; and that for England and Wales, later in 1846, by the Supreme Council for the Northern Jurisdiction of the United States.

There are also Supreme Councils in Canada, Portugal, Italy, Hungary, Greece, Switzerland, Brazil, Peru, Venezuela, Nueva Granada, Uruguay, the Argentine Confederation, Chile, Central America, Mexico, Egypt, and Cuba for the West Indies.

Everywhere, except in Great Britain, Canada, Chile, and the United States, the Supreme Councils administer all the Degrees, and the Inspectors confer the Blue Degrees, and establish Master's Lodges: and these are chartered and governed by the Supreme Councils. The Supreme Councils in the United States have never exercised these powers, leaving, for the sake of harmony, the Blue Degrees to be administered under the authority of the Grand Lodges, and themselves never chartering Symbolic Lodges.

The Supreme Councils originally consisted of nine members each; but in almost all the number has been enlarged. That of the Supreme Council for the Southern Jurisdiction of the United States is now fixed at thirty-three, who hold their office of Sovereign Grand Inspector-General for life. The officers of the Supreme Council also hold for life.

The Southern Jurisdiction of the United States consists of all the States except Maine, Massachusetts, Vermont, New Hampshire, Connecticut, Rhode Island, New York, New Jersey, Delaware, Pennsylvania, Ohio, Indiana, Illinois, Michigan, and Wisconsin. These were assigned to the Northern Council when it was created; and all the residue of the States and Territories of the United States were reserved to the Mother Council.

The Ancient and Accepted Scottish Rite is more widely ex- tended than any other system, no other being worked to any extent in the Latin Countries of Europe and America.

The laws by which it is governed are, 1°. The Constitutions and Regulations of the year 1762: 2°. The Statutes, Regulations, and Institutes adopted at different times, under these: 3°. The True Secret Institutes, or Grand Constitutions of the year 1786, which purport to have been enacted in that year by a Supreme Council of the 33d Degree, at Berlin, and approved and sanctioned by Frederick the Great, " Grand Patron, Grand Commander, Universal Grand Master, and True Defender of the Order : " and, 4°. The Constitutions and Statutes of the respective Supreme Councils. All these enactments of the 18th Century [original and translated] with its own Statutes and other documents, have been published by authority of the Supreme Council for the Southern Jurisdiction—the Grand Constitutions of 1786 being originally in Latin, and those of 1762, the Institutes , etc., in French.

The 33d Degree is conferred only by the Supreme Council. It is never applied for; but is given, upon unanimous election, to a limited number of persons in each State, as an Honorary Degree, the recipients becoming Honorary Members of the Supreme Council.

The Degrees, from the 1st to the 32d, are divided into six Temples or Classes, each administered by a body of the last Degree of the Class. The arrangement is as follows:

1. The Degree of Entered Apprentice: in French, Apprenti.
2. Fellow-Craft: in French, Compagnon.
3. Master Mason: in French, Maitre.

These Degrees are conferred by a Sovereign or Deputy Grand Inspector-General, or in and by a Symbolic Lodge. In the United States they are only conferred in the Lodge.

4. Secret Master.
5. Perfect Master.
6. Intimate [or Confidential] Secretary.

7. Provost and Judge.
8. Intendant of the Building.
9. Elected Knight [or Knight Elu] of the Nine.
10. Illustrious Elu of the Fifteen.
11. Sublime Knight Elu of the Twelve.
12. Grand Master Architect.
13. Knight of the Ninth Arch: or, Royal Arch of Solomon.
14. Grand Elect, Perfect and Sublime Mason.

These are styled the Ineffable Degrees, and are conferred in a Lodge of Perfection, of the 14th Degree.

15. Knight of the East; or, of the Sword.
16. Prince of Jerusalem.

These are conferred in a Council of Princes of Jerusalem, of the 16th Degree, distinct, or in the bosom of a Chapter of Rose-Croix.

17. Knight of the East and West.
18. Knight of the Eagle, Knight of the Pelican, or

Knight Rose-Croix [formerly styled Sovereign Prince Rose-Croix].

These are conferred in a Chapter of Knights Rose-Croix.

19. Grand Pontiff; or, Sublime Ecossais.
20. Grand Master of all Symbolic Lodges.
21. Patriarch Noachite; or, Prussian Knight.
22. Knight Royal Axe; or, Prince of Libanus.
23. Chief of the Tabernacle.
24. Prince of the Tabernacle.
25. Knight of the Brazen Serpent.
26. Prince of Mercy; or, Scottish Trinitarian.
27. Knight Commander of the Temple.
28. Knight of the Sun; or, Prince Adept.
29. Knight of St. Andrew of Scotland.
30. Knight Kadosh; or of the White and Black Eagle.

These Degrees are conferred either in a Council of Knights Kadosh, or in a Consistory of the 32d Degree.

31. Grand Inspector Inquisitor Commander.
32. Sublime Prince of the Royal Secret.

These Degrees are conferred either in the Grand Consistory of a State, or in a particular Consistory. Originally they were conferred by the Supreme Council only, or by its special authority; but that for the Southern Jurisdiction has now delegated the power to the Consistories.

The Supreme Council reserves to itself the power of conferring any or all of the Degrees; and even where there is a Grand Consistory, any active Member of the Supreme Council, or Special Deputy, has power to confer all, from the 4th to the 32d in- elusive.

The Grand Consistory in each State is the head and governing power, under the Supreme Council of the Kite in that State, grants Letters-Patent of Constitution for subordinate bodies, and receives dues from them; having legislative and appellate judicial powers.

It is only required that a candidate for the Ineffable and higher Degrees, even to the 33d, should be a Master Mason of some lawful Rite, and in good standing. No more can be required.

The Lodges of all the Degrees, from the 4th to the 14th in- elusive, are contained in the Lodge of Perfection. To open it, opens them all. But a Lodge, of any Degree, may be opened and closed independently. The case is the same with the bodies of the Degrees, from the 19th to the 29th, inclusive. They are all contained in a Council of Kadosh. Yet there is no reason why there may not be independent bodies of either of the Degrees; and as the 28th is the last Philosophical Degree, it would be more appropriate to give to bodies of that Degree jurisdiction over the Degrees from the 19th to the 27th, inclusive.

No Brother should be permitted to sit in a Lodge, unless properly clothed, with the Cordon, Apron, and Jewel of the Degree, or of a higher one.

The delays required to elapse between the Degrees are: Between 14th and 16th, 3 months.

"16th and 18th, 3"

"19th and 30th, 6"

"30th and 32d, one year."

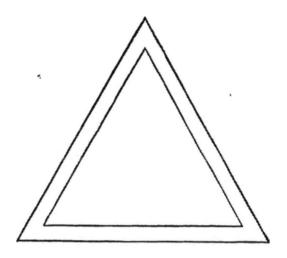

THE BLUE DEGREES.

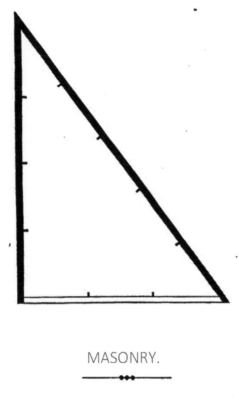

MASONRY.

DEFINITION AND OBJECTS OF, ETC.

Masonry, more appropriately called Free-Masonry, in French, Franc-Maçonnerie, in Latin, Latomia, or Lautumia, has received many definitions.

The definition given of the Order by the Grand Orient of France, is: "The Order of Frank-Masons is an association of wise and virtuous men, whose object is, to live in a perfect equality, to be intimately connected by the ties of esteem, confidence, and friendship, under the name of Brethren; and to stimulate each other to the practice of the virtues."

An English definition is, that "Freemasonry is a system of morality, vailed in allegory, and illustrated by symbols."

Each definition is exceedingly imperfect. The Order of Free- masons is, or ought to be, an association of intelligent, virtuous, disinterested, generous, and devoted men, regarding each other as Free,' Equals and Brothers, and bound by the obligations of fraternity to render each other mutual assistance. And Free- masonry is a system and school, not only of morals, but of political and religious philosophy, suggested by its allegories and concealed under its symbols. And, including in itself several Degrees of Knighthood, it is also a Chivalric Order, requiring the practice and performance of the highest duties of the man, the citizen, the patriot, and the soldier.

Intended to be all this, it has become denaturalized, not only by opening its doors too widely, so that all the multitude might rush in, but by becoming a mere association for mutual relief, and for inculcating ordinary principles of morality. The object of the Ancient and Accepted Scottish Rite is to restore to it its true character, as the apostle of the most lofty morality and virtue , of Freedom, with order; Equality, with due subordination ; Brotherhood, with reciprocal obligation ; political enlightenment and philosophical wisdom.

The definition of Masonry, in the Ancient and Accepted Scottish Rite [symbolized by the Square and Compasses], is : "A continuous advance, by means of the instruction contained in a series of Degrees, toward the Light, by the elevation of the Celestial, the Spiritual, and the Divine, over the Earthly, Sensual, Material and Human, in the Nature of Man "

THE LODGE, IT'S OFFICERS, DECORATIONS, ETC.

The officers of a Lodge are twelve in number. They are:

☉	1°. The Venerable Master.	Le Venerable Maitre.
⊕	2°. The Senior Warden	Le Premier Surveillant.
○	3°. The Junior Warden	Le Second Surveillant.
☿	4°. The Orator	L' Orateur.
▫	5° The Treasurer	Le Tresorier
△	6°.[2] The Secretary	Le Secretaire.
♂	7°. The Almoner.	Le Hospitalier, ou Aumonier.
♄	8°. The Senior Deacon, or Ex· pert	Le Premier Diacre, ou Expert.
♃	9°. The Master of Ceremonies	Le Maitre des Ceremonies.

---

[2] Sometimes the Secretariat is divided between two officers, the Keeper of the Seals, and the Keeper of the Archives.

♂	10°. The Junior Deacon, or Assistant expert	Le Second Diacre, ou Couvreur.
☿	11°. The Steward	Le Maitre des Refections.
⚔	12°. The Standard-Bearer	Le Porte-Etendart.

There is also always a Tiler (Tuilleur), on the outside of the entrance-door of the Lodge-room. . ↘ .

There may also be a Pursuivant, to be seated close to the door on the inside, and attend to alarms there. . ↗ .

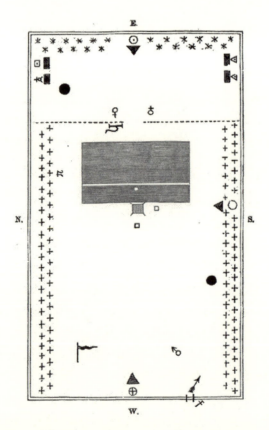

The Lodge is a rectangular parallelogram, about one-fourth of which is separated from the other three-fourths by a railing, and its floor is higher than that of the body of the Lodge, by three small steps. In the middle of the railing is an opening, nine feet wide. The railing should be made with small gilt rods and horizontal bars; from which blue curtains hang. The height of these should not be more than five feet.

The part of the hall so cut off from the rest, is, or is supposed to be, the eastern part of it. It is therefore called "The East, " or "The Orient." The principal entrance to the hall is always at the opposite end, or in the West.

The floor of the body of the Lodge represents a mosaic or tessellated pavement, being composed of alternate lozenges of black and white, with a wide bordering all round it, which, accommodating itself to the indentations of the lozenges, is, of course, " indented," or denticulated. The color of this bordering should be sky-blue.

At the extreme East is a platform, to which one ascends by three steps. On this is an arm-chair for the Venerable Master. In front of him is a triangular table, on which are to be a naked sword, a mallet, three lights, and implements for writing.

On each side of the Master's table should be a light, slender, fluted column, of the Composite order, an arch springing from one to the other. From the middle of the arch depends an equilateral triangle, of bars of yellow metal, in the centre of which, fixed by invisible wires, is the Hebrew letter י(Yud).

On the right of the Master, to the front, within the railing, is the Altar of Incense, a short, truncated, fluted column: and between the door and the South is the Altar of Ablutions, a like truncated column.

The Brethren at large sit on the North and South sides of the hall, the seats and brethren on each side being styled the "Column of that side. The Senior Warden sits in the extreme West, opposite the Master; and the Junior Warden on the South side, near to the wall, half-way the column of the South. Each sits on a platform raised one step, and has a table before him, like the Master's; and on each table are a sword, a mallet, and three lights. On each side the table of each is a column, those of the Senior Warden Corinthian, those of the Junior War- den Ionic.

All the tables, the altars, the seats, and the stool of the Altar of Obligations are covered with light-blue cloth; and curtains of the same extend to the floor in front of the tables of the three dignitaries. On each curtain of the Master's table is embroidered, in crimson, or painted, a Square; on each of those of the Senior Warden's, a Level; and on each of those of the Junior Warden's, a Plumb.

Toward the East is spread on the floor, at the proper time, the Tracing-Board of the Degree in which the Lodge may be working: a square or oblong cloth, painted on which are the symbols or emblems of the Degree.

On the west side of the Tracing-Board is the Altar of Obligation, square, and three and a half feet high, with a brazen plate covering the top, and horns or flames of brass at each corner. Upon this altar will always be the Holy Bible, the Square, and the Compasses, the latter always opened to sixty degrees.

On the east, south, and west sides of the Altar, respectively, must always be a lighted candle, the three forming an equilateral triangle. Each should be long and large, and of blue wax, the candlesticks upon slender pedestals about three feet in height.

There is room for a person to pass between the wall and the seats of the Senior and Junior Wardens, respectively; the same is the case with the Master's seat.

The walls of the Lodge should be hung from ceiling to floor with light-blue cloth. This must at least be the case with the East.

On each side of the entrance is a column, proportioned according to the dimensions given in the Bible, and consequently short and heavy in proportion to their diameters, if those dimensions, as given in the Book of Kings, are correct, i.e., 18 cubits in height, and the chapiters upon them 5 additional cubits, and the diameters 4 cubits. But in Chronicles the height is given as 35 cubits, making, with the chapiters, 40. The capitals should be carved as if formed of the seed-vessels of the lotus, covered with wreaths or chains and lace or net-work, and surmounted by pomegranates. The one on the South is called Yachin; that on the North, Bohaz, or Boaz.

In the centre of the mosaic pavement is a five-pointed Star, emitting rays.

Visitors entitled to do so, are seated in the East, on either side of the Master.
The seats of the other officers will appear by the plan given above; in which each is designated by the character prefixed to each on the list. There are oblong tables for two Secretaries, or one and his Assistant; and also one for the Treasurer, and one for the Orator.

On the Altar of Incense are a tripod, censers, and cups containing perfumes for burning. On that of Ablutions is a brazen laver, always containing pure water.

On the North side of the hall are four columns, two Tuscan, and two Doric, of the same height as those of the Wardens.

In addition to the Altar-lights, and those before the officers, there must be eleven portable lights, always ready for the reception of visitors.

The points of the Square upon the Altar must be toward the East; consequently, those of the Compasses toward the West. If the Lodge possesses a regular gavel of steel, it should also be on the Altar.

As the Tracing-Board or Painting contains the symbols of Freemasonry, it is always spread out when the Lodge is at work. The Deacons will spread it, while the Brethren are being clothed, before opening.

On the Treasurer's table will be two lights, implements for writing, the box of fraternal assistance or for contributions, and the clothing and insignia for the Candidate.

On the Secretary's table, besides his books and papers, two lights, the Register of Visitors, the Ballot-box, and the pouch of Propositions, which is a bag of velvet or silk, attached to a small hoop, and with a short handle.

The ceiling will represent the heavens. Over the East is painted a great sun shining; over the Senior Warden, a crescent moon; over the Junior Warden, a five-pointed star.

All around the wall, just below the ceiling, is painted, in French Lodges, a knotted cord or rope [la houppe dentelée], about six inches in diameter, with tassels dependent from it at each corner. The knots are eighty-one in number.

On the ceiling, also, particular stars and constellations are painted. In the centre, the three stars in the belt of Orion, and between them and the North-east, the Pleiades, and Hyades, and Aldebaran ; half-way between Orion and the North-west, Regulus, in Leo ; in the North, Ursa Major ; in the North-west, Arcturus ; West of Regulus, Spica Virginis; in the West, An- tares ; in the South, Fomalhaut. Over the East, also, is Jupiter, and over the West, Venus; Mercury close to the Sun; and Mars and Saturn near the centre of the ceiling. The stars in the belt of Orion, represent the number 3; the Hyades, 5; the Pleiades and Ursa Major, 7. The five royal stars are Aldebaran, Arcturus, Regulus, Antares, and Fomalhaut.

In the two first Degrees, the Master is styled "Venerable." The other Dignitaries and Officers are styled, simply, "Brother" and "Brethren"

In the third Degree, the Master is styled "Worshipful;" the Wardens, "Most Venerable;" and the Master Masons other than the three Dignitaries, "Venerable"

It is not allowable, in addressing or speaking of an Officer or Brother, in the Master's Lodge, to omit his proper title. The terms "Dear" and " Very Dear" prefixed to the word "Brother" or "Brethren " in addressing an Officer or Brother, or Officers or Brethren, are represented, in the Ritual, by the initials , "D∴", or "V∴ D∴".

The Jewels, or Badges of the Dignitaries and Officers are:

For the Master   A Square.

For the Senior Warden	A Level.
For the Junior Warden	A Plumb.
For the Orator	An Open Book, or a Roll.
For the Treasurer	Two Keys, crossed.
For the Secretary	Two Pens, crossed.
For the Almoner	An Open Hand.
For the Senior Deacon	A Gavel.
For the Master of Ceremonies	The Compasses, opened to 90 degrees, on the Arc of a Circle graduated.
For the Junior Deacon	The 24-inch Gauge.
For the Steward	Two Wands, crossed.
For the Standard-Bearer	A Pennon.
For the Pursuivant	An Arrow.
For the Tiler	A Sword.

If the Secretariat is divided:

For the Keeper of the Seals	A Signet Ring.
For the Keeper of the Archives	Two Pens, crossed.

Each Jewel is enclosed in a triangle, and the whole of silver.

The dress should be a black coat, black pantaloons, and black or white vest. Master Masons wear their hats in each of the Lodges.

The Clothing is a square Apron of white lambskin (not of cotton or linen), tied by a blue silk cord, which ends in front with tassels. The apron is entirely plain, without any emblems or devices, lined with light-blue silk, and edged with light-blue ribbon, no more or less than half an inch wide. The flap is cut to a point in the middle, and lined and edged like the main apron. The width and depth of the apron, fourteen inches.

The Dignitaries alone wear scarfs of light-blue silk. All Officers and Brethren wear swords, steel-hilted, with black belts round the body and black shoulder-straps. The scabbard is of black leather and steel-mounted.

All wear white gloves. These are part of the Clothing. They should be of silk or cotton.

VISITORS AND HONORS.

Every Lodge has a book, called "The Register of Visitors." Before the Lodge opens, this book is taken to the Ante-room, and no Visitor can be admitted until he has inscribed on the Register his name, his Lodge, if a member of one, and his office or rank. When all are inscribed, the book is taken into the Lodge.

In receiving Visitors, the lights taken out are termed Stars. Visitors are introduced in classes, and with the honors following:

Brethren of the three first Degrees, the Brethren standing, and under the Sign of Order.

Masons of the 14th Degree, with two Stars and two Swords.

The Princes of Jerusalem, 16th Degree, with three Stars and three Swords.

Knights Rose-Croix, Actual Masters of Blue Lodges, and Actual Presiding Officers of Lodges of Perfection and Councils of Princes of Jerusalem, with four Stars and four Swords.

Knights Kadosh and Actual Presiding Officers of Chapters of Rose-Croix, with five Stars and five Swords.

The Actual Commander of a Council of Kadosh, and Princes of the Royal Secret, with six Stars and six Swords, and Arch of Steel.

The Commander-in-chief of a Particular Consistory of the jurisdiction, or of a Grand Consistory, not of it, or a 32°, Deputy of the Supreme Council, with seven Stars and seven Swords, and Arch of Steel.

The Commander-in-Chief of the Grand Consistory of the jurisdiction, and all Deputies, of the 33d Degree, regularly commissioned by the Mother Supreme Council, and all Sovereign Grand Inspectors-General of the 33d Degree, other than those hereinafter mentioned, with eight Stars and eight Swords, and Arch of Steel.

All Active and Emeriti Members, not Dignitaries, of the Mother Supreme Council, and her Deputies for Louisiana, and Active Members of other Supreme Councils in alliance with the

Mother Supreme Council, with nine Lights and nine Swords, Steel Arch, Swords clashing and Mallets beating.

A Sov∴ Grand Commander of another jurisdiction, or a Past Sovereign Gr∴ Commander of any, or a Dignitary or Past Dignitary of the Sup∴ Council, with ten Stars and ten Swords, Steel Arch, Swords clashing and Mallets beating.

The Sov∴ Gr∴ Commander of the Mother Supreme Council , or his Special Delegate and Proxy, with eleven Stars and eleven Swords, Steel Arch, Swords clashing and Mallets beating.

But no honors are to be rendered to any Mason whose dignity or rank in the Ancient and Accepted Rite shall be inferior to that of the Presiding Officer; nor when the Commander-in-Chief of the Grand Consistory of the State shall already have been received and is present; except, in any case, when the visitor is an active member of the Supreme Council, or a Sovereign or Past Sovereign Grand or Lieut∴ Grand Commander, or the Special Delegate or Proxy of the Sovereign Grand Commander.

While receiving visitors entitled to honors, all the Brethren and the Officers, except the Master, will be uncovered. He uncovers to no one.

THE PROPOSING AND ELECTING OF MEMBERS.

No Profane[3] can be admitted who has not attained the age of twenty-one years, or who is not free-born, of free and not servile condition, respectable profession, trade, or employment, no atheist, nor in his dotage; or who is not master of his own per son and actions, of some degree of education, at least able to read and write, of good repute and well recommended.

No domestic or servant of any class can be admitted; no professional gambler; no person without visible means of decent support; no one following any low, vile, abject employment.

No monk or Jesuit can be admitted; nor any tool or instrument of any unlawful tyranny or usurpation.

No person whatever can, under any pretext, ever be admitted to a Degree, without full payment of the regular fee.

The final vote on the question of admission cannot be taken until the third meeting of the Lodge after and including that at which he is proposed.

---

[3] Profanus: a person profano, outside of the Temple—one not of "The Holy House of the Initiated." The word has no odious meaning.

The interval between proposal and initiation will regularly be three months ; but this may be reduced to forty-five days, if in that time there have been three meetings, with due notice of each to all the Brethren.

In every case the petition for admission of the Profane, written and signed by himself, will be presented, in the following form:

"To the Venerable Master, the Wardens, and Brethren of Lodge, No. —, of the State of , ¯of the Ancient and Accepted Scottish Rite of Freemasonry:

I, A B , being free by birth, and of the full age of twenty-one, do declare that, unbiased by any " solicitation of friends or others, and uninfluenced by mere " curiosity, or by mercenary or other unworthy motives, I freely " and voluntarily offer myself for the Mysteries of Freemasonry; " that I am prompted to do so by a favorable opinion conceived " of the Fraternity, the desire of knowledge, and a sincere wish " to be serviceable to my fellow-creatures ; and that I will cheer- " fully conform to all the ancient usages and established customs " of the Order. I am   years of age; was born at   , " in   ; am of the profession ['trade,' or 'employment' [of   ; and reside at .

AB, Recommended and vouched for by

C   D   ,

Member of the Lodge"

This petition is to be handed by the vouching Brother to the Venerable Master, in private. The voucher must not be given without a full and intimate acquaintance with the character, habits, and disposition of the candidate; and it applies as well to his intellectual as to his moral character. No man who is not possessed of the mental strength and ability to understand and value the instruction conveyed, some education, and some taste for study and capacity for reflection, ought to be allowed admission, even to the Lesser Mysteries. And if the voucher presents a drunkard, gambler, seducer, cheat, or unfair dealer, he must himself be expelled from the Order. The plea of ignorance will not excuse him. Everyone recommends and vouches as of personal knowledge, and accepts the risk.

The right of exercising one's judgment by the secret ballot is absolute. No Mason is bound to receive as his brother one whom he dislikes or suspects, or thinks unintelligent, or likely to be indolent, indifferent, or pragmatical. To question him for his vote, is to deserve expulsion; and the Lodge should always be content to retain a tried brother, when it must virtually lose him to acquire a stranger, unknown to it as Masons know each other.

If there be one or more other Lodges, of any regular Rite, in the place where, notice of an application for initiation will be given to each, as soon as it is made. Valid objections to a Profane may thereby become known, which would otherwise remain unrevealed.

Applications for affiliation will be made by petition, and will be acted on as the Statutes of the Lodge may prescribe.

REGULATIONS.

Each Lodge will frame and adopt its own Statutes, and its Rules of Business and Order. These will be at once in force. But they must be, within a brief space, submitted to the Grand Consistory of the State, or, if there be none, then to the proper Active or Deputy Inspector-General, that if they contain anything contrary to the Grand Constitutions, or to the Laws, Statutes, Ordinances, Canons, or Regulations of the Supreme Council, or of the Grand Consistory, if there be one, so much of them may be disapproved, and by such disapproval, when that is made known to the Lodge, cease to be of force, unless it be decided that such part or parts were, from the beginning, null and void.

The Statutes must provide that there shall be regular meetings of the Lodge on the days of the summer and winter solstice ; that is, on the 24th of June, the festival of the Nativity of St. John the Baptist, and on the 27th of December, the festival of the birth of St. John the Evangelist. On these days the Brethren will dine together. The election of officers will be held at the regular meeting next preceding the winter solstice; and they will be installed on that day.

The officers of Lodges will be elected for not less than three years. The first seven are elective officers. The others are appointed by the Master.

The right to Masonic burial cannot be denied to Fellow-Crafts and Entered Apprentices. They are Freemasons. Nor can it be allowed to Masons long unaffiliated, and long neglectful of their duties.

Either an Entered Apprentices' or Fellow-Crafts' Lodge may be separately opened; but when a Lodge of Master Masons is opened, it includes in itself both the other Lodges; and the work of the first may be suspended, to commence or resume work in either of the two last.

APARTMENTS CONNECTED WITH THE LODGE.

There must be a convenient and comfortable Ante-room (Salle de pas perdus) for the reception of visitors and other necessary purposes. It must be a room, one door opening into the Lodge-room, and with another door for exit, that may be kept closed.

There must also be a Preparation-room, with a door opening into the Lodge-room on the left of the Senior Warden. Here candidates will be prepared; and here also visitors may await admission.

In the Ante-room must be a desk, with materials and implements for writing, on which desk the Register of Visitors will be laid. In this room, also, the wardrobe should be kept, and a book for subscriptions for banquets and festivals. It should be well supplied with chairs, and one or more tables for writing.

In the Preparation-room there will be no furniture, except a single table, some chairs, and a book-case or cases containing the library. The following sentences are painted on the wall, or are suspended, in large print, and framed, in a conspicuous place:

"If mere curiosity brings thee hither, turn back, begone!"

"If thou fearest to see the faults and frailties of humanity dissected, thou wilt find no satisfaction amongst us"

"If thou valuest worldly goods and advantages alone, thou wilt find nothing here to aid thee in thy purpose"

"If thou lackest confidence in us, advance no further!"

"If thy heart be pure, and thy intentions good, thou art welcome!"

"If thou per severest, thou wilt be purified by the Elements; thou wilt emerge from the abyss of darkness, and see the Light"

* * * * * *

"Dust we are, and unto dust we must return"

"In the grave all men are equal"

"He that goeth down to the grave shall come up no more"

"The way of the wicked is as darkness.   They know not at what they stumble"

"He that walks with the wise shall be wise; but the companion of fools shall be destroyed"

"He who stops his ears at the cry of the poor, shall himself cry and not be heard"

"Remove not the old land-marks; and enter not into the fields of the fatherless"

"He that has no rule over his own spirit, is a city dilapidated and without walls"

"Hell and destruction are never full."

"God shall judge the righteous and the wicked"

*   *   *   *   *   *

ORDER OF BUSINESS.

The regular order of business in every Lodge of the Rite is:

1. The reading and signing of the records of the previous communication or communications, as yet unread and unsigned, which are entered in a book, called "The Book of Architecture." To insure the correctness of the entries, and avoid the necessity of defacement by erasures and interlineations, the minutes of each meeting are kept on loose sheets, called "plates," and are invariably to be read over while in the rough, just before the closing of the communication at which they are taken, that any error or omission may at once be corrected, before the formal record is made up.
2. Report from the Bro∴ Almoner, of any special case or cases, requiring relief or assistance.
3. Reports from Permanent or Standing Committees.
4. Reports from Special or Select Committees.
5. Applications for Initiation, Reception, or Admission to Membership.
6. Consideration of previous Proposals for Initiation or Affiliation.
7. Receptions.
8. Motions and Resolutions.

Alter Reports from Committees are received, their consideration, if they give rise to debate, may be postponed until after the Initiations or Receptions.

At every meeting the Secretary will place before the Master the "Order of the Day," on which, under the above heads, will be stated the different matters to be considered and acted upon. The Lodge may postpone any matter, by "passing to the Order of the Day."

MISCELLANEOUS.

1. All trials for offenses must be held in open Lodge, before the whole Lodge, on regular charges and specifications, the vote on each of which will be taken separately, by yeas

and nays, the youngest member, not an officer, voting first, and so on up to the eldest, and then the officers, beginning with the Tiler and ending with the Master. The punishments are, censure or reprimand; fines; pecuniary restitution; suspension from member- ship or the privileges of Masonry for a definite or indefinite time; expulsion from the Lodge, and deprivation of the character of Mason. Suspension for an indefinite time can only be terminated by vote of three-fourths of all the Brethren present at a regular meeting, taken upon a call of names, beginning with the youngest Mason, and after notice given at the preceding regular meeting. Three Brethren may demand a Committee of Inquiry before the ballot. Suspension for a definite period will terminate at the end of the period, unless it is continued by vote of three-fourths of the Brethren present, taken in the same manner , at a regular meeting, after notice by a Brother, and demand for it, at the preceding regular meeting. The notice and demand will continue the suspension until the ballot. Three Brethren may demand a Committee of Inquiry; and the suspension should be continued, if the suspended party have not reformed or made reparation. If continued, it becomes indefinite. A majority of three-fourths is necessary to expel; a simple majority of votes will suspend.

2. A Lodge can never close until the box of fraternal assistance is sent around; and no Brother can withdraw from the Lodge before it closes, without depositing his contribution. The sum contributed will be handed to the Almoner, to be used in relieving distress. It may be directed to be applied to a particular case, of a party named or unnamed, on motion of any Brother. However applied, the party relieved is never to be in- formed from what source the relief comes.

3. A Lodge cannot be "called off" until another day or evening. When at refreshment, the members remain in presence of the Junior Warden, on whose table the small gilt column of Harmony is then placed upright.

4. The Lodge must always be opened and closed in due and proper form. No openings "without form" or "in short" are allowable.

5. No Brother can leave the Lodge before it closes, without permission from the Senior Warden, which will only be given for good cause. Any Brother may object to another leaving, and demand a vote of the Lodge; which ought not to permit withdrawal, except for good cause, since thereby the most important business is often transacted by a few, or neglected.

6. The Brethren will always be called to order precisely at the hour and moment fixed. Brethren arriving afterward must render good excuse, or be liable to censure and even to fine.

7. The Banner of the Lodge is to be of white silk, edged and fringed with blue. On one side, embroidered or painted in blue and gold, the Square and Compasses; and on the other the Blazing Star of five points. Over the Square and Compass, the motto " Maçonnerie Oblige :" and over the Blazing Star, the words, in Hebrew, אלהים אלוהינו

[Yarat Alohim], meaning "Reverence for the Deity." The banner should be square, each side measuring about thirty inches; and it should be attached to a light staff, as below, with a spear-head above.

8. There are no assemblies of Masons, in the Ancient and Accepted Rite, "working after the manner of a Lodge." Masons can only be made in " just and regularly constituted Lodges of such." In a State where there is a Grand Consistory, Letters of Constitution for Lodges will be granted by that body. The Commander-in-Chief or an Inspector-General or Deputy may grant temporary Letters, to be confirmed or revoked by the Grand Consistory. If these are confirmed, Letters of Constitution issue, confirming and making perpetual the temporary Letters. Where there is no Grand Consistory, Letters of Constitution are granted by an Inspector-General, or Deputy, on which Letters-Perpetual issue as of course. In every case, Officers must at the beginning be elected and duly invested with office by installation; to hold their offices until the Winter solstice occurring not less than two years and a half, nor more than three years and a half afterward.

9. If the Master be absent at any meeting, a Past Venerable Master, Prince of the Royal Secret, or Inspector-General, must be called on to preside. The Senior Warden does not take the Master's place, of right, or by succession, and will preside only when no Past Master, Prince of the Royal Secret, or Inspector-General is present. In the absence of these, and of the Senior Warden, the Junior Warden will preside. If none of these are present, a Knight Rose-Croix may preside, if he have received also the 20th Degree. In the absence of all these, no Lodge can be held.

10. An appeal to the Lodge may be taken from any decision of the Master, except on questions of order; and on them, when the question whether a Brother is in order depends for its solution on some land-mark or essential principle of Freemasonry.

11. The Master may, at any moment, close a debate by rising to his feet and rapping once.

12. Masons of the Ancient and Accepted Bite will use, after initials and abbreviations, three dots, forming an equilateral triangle, thus: "Ven∴" . . . "A∴ M∴", instead of the period.

13. Official letters and documents will be dated as follows :

"O∴ OF .

"The   day of the Hebrew month   ,

"A∴ M∴   , answering to the   day of

"V∴ E∴ 187—."

The initial O∴ stands for Orient. The name of the Hebrew month may be written in Hebrew or English. The initials V∴ E∴ mean "Vulgar or Ordinary Era;" and are to be used instead of A∴ D∴

Each Secretary must annually procure, and always keep in his office, a calendar of the Hebrew months for the year.

The Hebrew year begins with the month תשרי Tisri, which commences on some day in September. To find the Hebrew year, before that day in September, add 3760 to the current year. After that day, add 3761.

14. All the ordinary business and family affairs of the Lodge are transacted in the Degree of Entered Apprentice. All banquets are held in that Degree.
15. A Knight Rose-Croix, and of course a Mason of higher Degree, is not " tiled" that is, examined by the catechism, but is admitted on his brief or patent, and verification of his signature. Nevertheless, should he be unable to give the word, at the opening of a Fellow-Craft's or Master's Lodge, or otherwise be reasonably suspected of not being what he seems, he may be strictly tiled.
16. Every Brother entering the Lodge after it is opened, will salute the three Dignitaries in succession, with the Sign, beginning with the Master.

מדרגה אחת

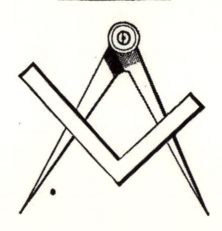

First Degree

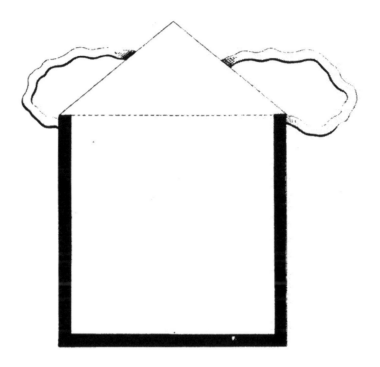

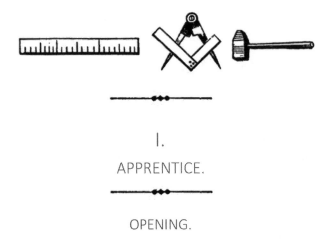

I.
APPRENTICE.

OPENING.

···

The Tiler is at his post, to guard against the approach of all cowans and eavesdroppers, on the hills or in the vales; and to see that none enter the Lodge except such as are duly entitled, and have the permission of the Venerable Master.

···

The Junior Warden occupies the South, the better to observe the Sun at his meridian height, to send the workmen to their labors, and recall them from work to refreshment, that the Venerable Master may have honor and glory thereby.

···

As the Sun sets in the West to close the day, so is the Senior Warden in the West to close the Lodge, to pay the workmen, and send them away content and satisfied.

···

As the Sun rises in the East to begin his course and open the day, so is the Venerable Master in the East to open the Lodge, to direct it in its work, and to enlighten it with his knowledge.

···

In the name of God, and of St. John of Scotland, and under the auspices of the Supreme Council (Mother-Council of the World), of the Sovereigns, the Grand Inspectors- General, Grand Elect Knights of the Holy House of the Temple, Grand Commanders of the Holy Empire, of the 33d and last Degree of the Ancient and Accepted Scottish Kite of Freemasonry, for the Southern Jurisdiction of the United States, whose See is at Charleston, in the State of South Carolina,. . . [Or, if there be a Grand Consistory in the State] ... of the Grand Consistory of Sublime Princes of the Royal Secret, 32d Degree of the Ancient and Accepted Scottish Rite of Freemasonry, for the State of; and by virtue of the authority in me vested as Venerable Master of this Lodge of Apprentice Masons, I declare it to be duly opened, and its labors in full force. No Brother may speak aloud, or pass from one Column to the other, without first obtaining permission; or may engage in political questions or controversy; under the penalties prescribed by the General Statutes of the Order.

....

ENGRAVED PLATE OF WORKS OF THE LAST COMMUNICATION READ.

....

INTRODUCTION OF VISITORS.

....

☉∴ Brethren, we congratulate ourselves on our good fortune in being visited by you, and cordially offer you the poor hospitalities of our Temple. We fully appreciate the value of your presence among us, and especially on the present occasion . . . [giving the reasons]. With our numbers thus enlarged, we may labor more effectually and impressively; and shall be assisted and strengthened in inculcating and propagating the principles of Virtue and Fraternity, which the Ancient and Accepted Scottish Rite professes. Be seated among us, Brethren! Brother Master of Ceremonies, conduct our worthy and well-beloved Brethren to appropriate seats.

*　　*　　*　　*　　*
....

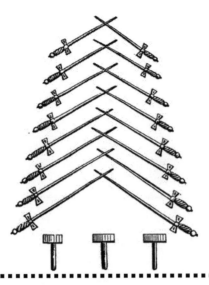

⊙∴ Brethren, we hail with joy and welcome your entrance into this Temple of Harmony and Virtue, to participate in our labors. We thank you for the encouragement thus given by you to the workmen of this Lodge, and especially to the young and the Apprentices of the Craft, whose zeal and ardor in Masonry will naturally be stimulated by this proof that our labors are not uninteresting to others, even to the most distinguished and illustrious of the great Fraternity ; and in whom a praiseworthy ambition will also be aroused at sight of the due honors paid to high rank and long service in the Royal Art Be indulgent, Brethren, in respect to aught you may see amiss or imperfect in our work. Aid us with your wise counsel and ad- vice; since it is the duty of every Mason of intelligence to dispense light and knowledge among the uninformed Brethren. You are welcome, Brethren. My Brethren of the Lodge, aid me in welcoming these Brethren more appropriately, in the universal language of Masonry.

RECEPTION.

You have asked to be admitted to the Temple of Freemasonry. To attain what you desire, you must submit to its laws, and undergo the tests of initiation into the Ancient Mysteries, the tests of the four ancient elements. The first is of the Earth. You will undergo it here seated on that to which the bodies of men are sooner or later committed. "The way of life is above to the wise that he may depart from the hell beneath."

When I leave you, carefully survey and explore the place in which you are! Read what is written on its walls! Re- fleet! Pause! Debate with yourself! If your life has been innocent, or, when not so, its faults repented of; if your heart is pure, and your motives laudable, and your courage firm— Proceed! Otherwise, Depart! And seek to know no more. "He who comes in with vanity, departs in darkness, and his name shall be covered with darkness."

••

Qu∴

••

1°. "Man, compounded of a body and a soul, owes duties to himself as each. What are those duties?"

2°. "What duties does man owe to his fellow-creatures?"

3°. "What duties does man owe to his country; and what is he bound, in her distress, or to defend her honor, to sacrifice upon the altar of the commonwealth?"

4°. "What duties does man owe to his Creator?"

———

W∴

••

P... Tour probation is not yet over. We are not sure of your sincerity. Eat of the bread and drink of the water before you! They are the food of the victims of temporal and spiritual tyranny. Before you, also, are salt, Sulphur, and mercury, the three principles of our Brothers, the Alchemists, with which to perform The Great Work. To separate and unite are the great processes of the universe. Man is threefold, of body, mind, and spirit conjoined. The salt, sulphur, and mercury, are their symbols. Taste of the salt! The bodies of the dead, dissolving, and their particles become parts of the bodies of the living. Burn a little of the sulphur! Its flame and smoke are symbols of your good and evil thoughts. Take of the mercury in your hand, and seek to divide it into portions, these remaining near each other! The spirit is simple and indivisible. Reflect and learn!

••

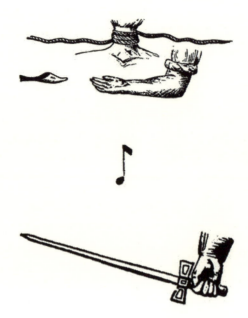

⊙∴ Since he is a Man—free-born, and of good repute— demand of him his name, the place of his birth, his age, his religion, his office, profession, or occupation, and the place of his present residence.

☉∴ Consider well, sir, what it is you ask. You do not know the dogma or the objects of the Ancient Order to which you seek to surrender yourself. It is not merely a Society for mutual relief, and to dispense charities within a limited outer circle.

When any Society has the strength of numbers, it necessarily owes duties, as a Society, to The Country, far higher than those which the members owe to each other. To fail to perform those duties, is to abdicate; and the non-performance, long-continued, becomes chronic impotence. For a long time, not only most Societies, but most individuals, have failed to perform their highest duties to their country, exclusively engaged, as they have been, in selfishly caring for their own interest and welfare.

The Order into which you now ask to enter acknowledges its responsibilities, its duties to the Country, its duties to Humanity, the necessity for progress. Thus it has the right of demanding the performance of grave duties and stern sacrifices of its Initiates. It has fore-shadowed to thee what these duties may be; what the ex- tent of these sacrifices. Tour descent into the bowels of the earth, your confinement in the dungeon, are typical of, and shadow forth both. The sword near your heart indicates also one sacrifice that may become necessary; as well as the punishment of those who refuse to follow out the inexorable rectilinear logic of Duty, and to obey the man- dates of a despotic Patriotism. Death, or a grave in exile is an acceptable alternative for devotion; and the true name of devotion is disinterestedness. We are but atoms of the great aggregate which constitutes that fraction of the unit of Humanity, our Country. We are the leaves on the great tree. What though the leaves fall upon the roots! Will not the tree still continue to grow? The calamities of the Present are the terrible price of the Future. From the pressure of all desolation, Faith gushes forth. Sufferings bring their agony, and ideas their immortality. These mingle, and compose death. He who dies in the performance of duty, dies in the radiance of the Future, and enters a grave illuminated by the Dawn.

It is always for the ideal, and for the ideal alone, that those devote themselves who do devote themselves. Men sacrifice themselves for visions, which, to the sacrificed, are almost always illusions, but illusions with which, upon the whole, all human certainties are mingled.

The preparation by Abraham to sacrifice his only legitimate son, is a grand and sublime allegory. So a country or a society must place its children on the altar, when the coming generations demand it.

We have spoken to you of……… The Order will demand one of you…….. It has been.... by many of the best and foremost men that ever lived. By their lives and deeds, you may know to what the Ancient and Accepted Scottish Rite prompts and stimulates its Initiates. Nor is that obligation all. The Roman youth, in the days before Octavius, saw daily in the atrium of his habitation the marble statues of his ancestors, and was thereby daily taught and obligated to imitate their virtues, and emulate their heroic deeds. He is a traitor to a heroic ancestry, who is not himself heroic. The old French said, "Noblesse oblige with us, "Maçonnerie oblige" It is our motto: Masonry is Obligation. He is a traitor to Masonry, who does not do the duties of a Mason, into whatever calamity that may lead him. He might justly be dealt with by the sword or the cable-tow; and of this, the Let the feeling of each be never effaced from your memory!

Sightless and helpless, you know your rights as a man, since by being such you assert a claim to enter here. Yet you are at the mercy of you know not whom. Sad type of a people, blind, bound, and defenseless, with the three- fold cord of oppression around its neck!

This Order had its birth in that mysterious Orient which is yet an enigma to the Profane; and its roots reach back to the remote past. It is the growth or the ruin of centuries. It is a Sphynx. The (Edipus who attempts to solve the enigma and fails, or half-succeeds, dies, the victim of inexorable Fate. You have passed through the first test of the Ancient Initiations, that of the Earth. Its pitiless rigor has been softened, so that it remains but a symbol of what it was. Others are to follow, to bear which without faltering will require all your courage. Are you resolved to submit to them? Have you the courage to brave all the possible dangers to which that resolution may expose you?

⊙∴ Once again I warn you to reflect If you become a Freemason, of the Ancient and Accepted Scottish Kite, you will find the stern realities of duty behind its symbols. You must not only war against and subdue your own passions, but you must in earnest strive and strike to overcome other foes of Humanity—the hypocrites who deceive it, the faith- less who defraud, the fanatics who oppress it; the ambitious who usurp upon it, and the corrupt and unprincipled who make profit of the confidence of the masses. One does not war against these without personal danger. Have you the energy, the resolution, the devotion, to engage in that life- long warfare against darkness, perfidy, and error?

⊙∴ It is thus, through dangers and difficulties, that men attain initiation. So do false Philosophies and specious, plausible Creeds, pretending to be Brethren of the Light, drag down the soul that listens to them into the pits of error. Though Masonry, sir, is not a Religion, and pro- claims absolute freedom of conscience, still it has a Creed; and Masons agree that one ought not to engage in any important undertaking, without first invoking the assistance of The Grand Architect of the Universe.

ORISONS.

Grand Architect of all that hath a place,

In the illimitable realms of space,

To whom Humanity it's being owes—

The One, from Whom the Manifold outflows—

Benignly hear our earnest, humble prayer,

And over us extend Thy watchful care!

Help us, Thy faithful workmen, to fulfill,

In this our work-shop, Thy majestic will!

In this great warfare which we here maintain,

Over our passions let our reason reign!

And let that reason, humbled, evermore,

Bow reverently the Godlike Truth before!

Be Thou, oh Father! Guardian and guide Of this Profane, blind, feeble, and untried!

Help him the ills of life to overcome,

And let him find the Lodge a happy home!

PRAYER.

Our Father, who art in heaven! We humble ourselves before Thee, the sovereign Arbiter of all the worlds. We recognize Thy infinite power and our infinite feebleness. Help us to contain our hearts and souls within the limits of righteousness; and enable us, journeying by safe ways, to elevate ourselves toward Thee, the grand Architect and Lord of the universe! Thou art One, and self-existent; to Thee every created thing owes its being. Thy energy acts in everything and through everything; and, invisible to every creature, Thou seest all things. Thee alone we invoke, and to Thee alone we address our prayers.

Deign, oh grand Architect, to protect the peaceful workmen whom Thou seest here assembled! Make more ardent their zeal and devotion! Strengthen their souls in the arduous struggle against their passions; fill their hearts with the love of virtue, and enable them to overcome! So also enable this aspirant, who desires to partake of our august Mysteries. Lend him Thy aid, and uphold him now and always, in all trials and perplexities, in all dangers and difficulties, with Thy omnipotent arm! Amen!

■■

☉∴ What thoughts occurred to you, when

Answer frankly! You will not offend us.

■■

☉∴ We have already in part indicated to you for what purpose you were submitted to the first test—that of the Earth. The ancients held that there were four elements, Earth, Air, Water, and Fire. That they were mistaken in these being elements, or the simple principles of things, in no way interferes with the symbolism which connected itself with them, and has come down to us ; since the Truths em- bodied in that symbolism are genuine and immortal. The Kabalah of the Hebrews, and our brethren the Alchemists and Hermetic philosophers, also recognized these as the four elements; and aspirants to Initiation have in all ages been tested by each.

You were surrounded by emblems of mortality and the written utterances of wisdom; firstly, to compel serious and solemn reflection, the proper preparative of a step so momentous as Initiation into the Mysteries. It was hoped that you would remember that the dungeon has ever been one of the chief instruments of tyranny, whether of the despot or the prelate: that in the middle ages, the castles of the nobles were ever reared on the arches of dungeons; that the Inquisition had its dark cells for its victims; and that the Bastile was but one among hundreds of prisons, built by kings, or tyrants like those of Venice, and tenanted by those who were deemed dangerous or suspicious, who were in the way of a royal or noble amour, or who had in their keeping a perilous secret.

And we hoped that you, remembering this, would be inspired with a pious anger against all despotisms, over the body or the conscience; and with a more fervent love for such free institutions of government as forbid the imprisonment of a Galileo for announcing a physical fact, and that of a Hampden or a Sydney for proclaiming political truths so rudimental that they are now taught as axioms to children.

The first act of an oppressed people, asserting its right, under God's patent, to freedom, is to destroy the bastilles which were the pride and safety of their imperious masters. We hoped that you would reflect that it could not but be the duty of a society of intelligent men, to do its utmost to release the prisoners unjustly confined in dungeons of stone and iron; but also to demolish the bastilles, stronger than those material ones, in which ignorance and error, superstitions and prejudices keep manacled the spirits, the intellects, and the consciences of so vast a majority of the great human family.

Remembering, too, how the dungeon had often been more ennobled than the throne and the altar, by the presence and even immolation there of the noble victims of tyranny; how great works of intellect had been written there; how often their doors, turning on the harsh hinges, had opened, only to send the wise, the great, and the good to the pyre or the scaffold, we had the right to hope that you too would resolve to maintain the sacred cause of freedom and toleration, even at the risk of incarceration, and of a lifetime spent in solitude and darkness. The cell of the martyr of liberty is irradiated with a holy light; the dungeon of the victim of spiritual despotism retains the traces of the consoling presence of the Holy Spirit of God.

The emblems of mortality around you could not but teach you to reflect on the instability and brevity of human life. But that, by itself alone, is a trite lesson, daily taught, and ever disregarded. You should also have reflected of how little value is that which is so short, and held by so uncertain a tenure, when weighed in the scales against duty and honor; and how infinitely mean is an ignoble, useless, idle life, in comparison with a glorious death, or with benefits conferred on one's country, or one's fellows, at the risk of life.

Orpheus, the Grecian allegory said, descended into the gloomy shades of the infernal regions; and Virgil makes Æneas to do the same. The Candidate in the Ancient Initiations did so, and saw represented many of the Tartarean horrors. Initiation was constantly termed "a new birth" "regeneration;" and to be born again it was deemed that one must first descend into the grave. Of that, the cave into which you were dragged is symbolical If you desire to become a true Mason, you must first die to vice, errors, and vulgar prejudices, and be born again, ascending through the Seven Spheres over which the Seven Arch- angels preside, to Virtue, Honor, and Wisdom—to manliness, in short—the synonyme of the Roman word for virtue.

In whatever you see or hear in Masonry, you will find a meaning. If it is hidden from you, search, and you shall find it every symbol, and all the ceremonial are replete with significance, and have a reason for being found here. Let those who deem our ceremonies idle and ridiculous, still think so. "Cast not your pearls before swine," the Master said, "lest they trample them under their feet, and turn again and rend you" The Mason to whom Freemasonry is not a grave and serious affair, is a false Mason, and if anything in the ceremonial seems absurd or trivial, it seems so only to ignorance, which we are glad to enlighten, or to self-conceit, which is not worth enlightening.

Let me also caution you against imagining that we scoff at religious creeds. You will learn the creed of Masonry hereafter. Know, meanwhile, that although we deem no homage more worthy of God, than Candor, Science, and Virtue; and although we admit into the bosom of our Order all men possessed of those gifts, whatever their religion;—though the Christian, the Hebrew, the Mahometan, and the Pagan, like Socrates, and Cicero, and Plato, may meet around our altars as brethren; and the Holy Bible is of the furniture of a Christian Lodge alone, still we are neither hostile nor indifferent to religion, nor seek to set Masonry in its place. There is no antagonism or rivalry between the altars of the two. They may well and fitly stand side by side; if intolerance do not minister at those of religion.

Nor are you to imagine that we are the enemies of Government or the constituted Authorities, if that be just, and these worthy of honor. We censure and impeach only that which is wrong and hurtful; that, in government, which degrades man, and abases the dignity of human nature. But woe to the Mason who permits himself to become the instrument of tyranny, the supporter of usurpation, and the apologist for injustice, and for contempt for the laws and constitutions which contain the eternal guarantees of Liberty.

…………. Do you believe in One Supreme Being?

■ ■

This belief, creditable as it is to your heart, is not the exclusive patrimony of the philosopher, but is also possessed by the savage. Yet this is true in only a limited sense. For though the barbarian feels that he is not self-existent, and seeks in nature the Cause and Author of existence, his God is always in nature, his idol is his God, and his ideas of the Deity being wholly confused and false, he does not really believe in God, but in a something above him, which is not God, but an idol of the mind. Little more correct are the ideas of a large proportion of the civilized world. Only a few really believe and feel assured that there is a Deity, without form or local habitation, to Whom everywhere is Here, and every when is Now; beneficent, tender, merciful, loving, pitiful:—an Infinite Wisdom as well as Infinite Power; Whose laws are not the mandates of His will, but the expression of His nature; not right because He enacts them; but which His will enacts because they are right, and could not be His laws. Of the existence of the Supreme Deity we have the same evidence as we have of that which exists and thinks in other men and in ourselves. We know the Soul, when we know its utterances, its actions, its effects. In the same manner we know there is a GOD. The Universe is His manifestation. It, we are sure, does not reflect and think. Thought and speech prove the existence of the Soul. The Universe is the Book of God, in which His thoughts are registered; and by it we know Him and His nature. He speaks to the soul by its spheres, phenomena and events, its greatnesses and its littlenesses, and within our souls as well as without Nature is the primitive revelation. Science enlarges our knowledge of God, because it translates for us more of His language, and translates it more truly.

Philosophy is the interpreter of nature, the Revealer: and Masonry consists in Morality, Science, Philosophy, and Political and Religious Truth. The Supreme Will and Intelligence is a personal God.

.... What do you understand by the word Virtue?

••

Virtue is an attribute and disposition of the mind, from which flows effort to overcome or govern the appetites and passions. It is, we have already said, in its primitive meaning, manliness. For the word Vir, in the Latin, meant a man, not merely one fraction of humanity, which was expressed by the word homo, a human creature; but a true, real, genuine Man. The man is Virtuous, who is not without desires, appetites, instincts, and passions; but who is master of and controls them. For virtue to exist, there must be a struggle and a warfare. The tame, spiritless, passionless, negative being is not virtuous. Virtue, therefore, is not to be confounded with honesty, benevolence, or even charity, or, calling it by its better name, loving-kindness. For honesty belongs often to the mere apathetic and untempted; benevolence to negativeness, weakness, and imbecility; and kindliness to those who are in many other respects vicious. Virtue is strong, vigorous, active, impassioned, more sublime in proportion to the energy of the passion it over- comes. To deprive ourselves of that which we value or need, in order to make the unfortunate happy, to incur personal danger or discomfort in order to defend the weak against the powerful, the unpopular against the popular, the losing cause against the winning, to toil for others or the country, without the hope of fee or reward, is virtue; and to sacrifice one's-self for the country or humanity, is to attain the highest eminence of virtue; an eminence which the poorest citizen or private soldier may reach. Nor is there any pleasure so great and true as that which attends and follows a victory over our own instincts, appetites, or passions. To be virtuous is to be happy; and if it were not, happiness is not the chief end of man's existence. To be happy and contented is a privilege bestowed on the animals. To be satisfied with one's-self, even in misery, is the privilege of a nature in which the human and divine are intermingled.

.... What do you understand by the word Vice?

••

Vice is the absence or opposite of virtue; as darkness, its symbol, is the absence or opposite of Light, the symbol of virtue. It is that disposition and attribute of the soul which produces the habit of satisfying our desires, and by means of which our appetites, and animal instincts, and baser passions continually gain strength, and at last become irresistible. As the habit of the virtuous man is to obey the dictates of conscience, of that universal conscience which is the Very

Truth, because it is an emanation from the Eternal Wisdom, so the vicious man offends against the dictates of that conscience, repents, and again offends, until he at last comes to disregard them altogether, and defy them. It is to impose salutary restraints on the impetuous rush of the appetites, to rise above the vile interests that trouble the weak Profane, to calm the feverish ardor of the passions, to learn the lofty truths of a sublime philosophy, and teach those truths to one another, and to unfold the wings of the soul to the pure and noble affections only, that we meet in our Masonic Temples. We work indefatigable here to attain unto sound and solid ideas of glory and virtue ; and regulating our conduct by the eternal principles of rational morality, and those rules of Duty and Eight which an enlightened conscience prescribes, we educate our souls to attain that just equilibrium of force and sensibility which constitutes the Wisdom and Perfection of Humanity .

But this is no easy task, to be accomplished without laborious effort, in a week, or a month; it is to create a habit that shall be a second nature. Yet it is this task to which you must devote yourself incessantly, until success crowns the work, if you persist in your determination to be received a Mason.

Perhaps you have come here a captive to very different ideas,—possibly a slave to the false and gross notions of depraved and illy-educated intellects. If to toil earnestly and incessantly in order to attain moral perfection, seems to you an undertaking beyond your strength, you are yet at liberty to return the way you came. If, on the other hand, you feel yourself equal to what Masonry will demand of you, say so. In either case, be frank and true, as becomes an honorable man!

⋯⋯

☉∴ Every association, Sir, has its peculiar laws, and every member has duties to perform; and, as it would be to him by the ties of blood-relationship, makes him guilty of an act of faithlessness, and dishonors him; to refuse to assist a Brother, is perjury; and true friendship, tender and consoling, is worshiped in our Temples, less because it is a sentiment, than because, being a duty, it may become and be made a virtue.

The third obligation, which you will not contract until after your initiation, will be to conform at all points to the ancient landmarks and general statutes of the Order, and to the particular laws of your Lodge; submitting your — self to whatsoever shall, in its name, be legally demanded of you; and to obey the constitutional and legal mandates and edicts of your lawful Chiefs in Masonry.

Now, Sir, you know what are the principal duties of a Mason. You may say that Masons, too generally, do not perform these duties; that their charities are small, and rarely bestowed; that their moneys, received for initiations and by contributions, are spent in show and parade ; that they rarely assist or advise each other; that they de- fame and malign one another; that rival rites and rival bodies quarrel; that Masons prove to be no better and no wiser than other men ; and that a Mason is often the last man to whom a Mason will apply for assistance, in distress, or for encouragement and support, when maligned or persecuted . You may, therefore, say to yourself, that the obligations of the Order are unreal, and its pretensions unfounded; and that you, too, may safely take those obligations, because you may, with the same impunity as others, neglect or violate them.

In part, at least, this is true. The populace has invaded the sanctuaries, and the true initiation, in the prevailing and popular Bite, has died out It has its Lodges in every little, obscure corner. It teaches little to its Initiates, and requires little of them. Too often it receives anyone who offers, in order to supply its treasuries. Even its Higher Degrees have ceased to be exclusive. Populous beyond example, it is powerless. Teaching morality only, it has ceased, even in that, to enforce its lessons; and the well-intentioned, knowing that the great majority of those whom they call their Brethren, will not perform their obligations to them, cease to consider themselves bound to succor or assist that majority. Thus it is that Masonry has ceased to exist there, except for the excellent and enlightened few, who lament, but cannot cure the deadly disease of which the Order dies, decaying at the root, and hollow, while fuller of leaf than ever.

It is because such is the condition of Masonry, that the authorities of the Ancient and Accepted Scottish Rite have resolved to form select bodies of Masons, by initiation according to their own forms, and by selection of the best from among Master Masons already made such in the other Rites; and within this limited circle to insist on the full performance of all Masonic duty; to lop off, without mercy, all dead and decayed branches, and no longer to permit the presence of the faithless, the lukewarm, or the apathetic in their Temples. Here, Masonic obligations are serious, solemn, and real. Imagine not that they can be lightly taken, and as lightly disregarded, with impunity. It would be a fatal mistake.

■■

הנרר מסתר.

■■

All men drink of the cup of good and evil fortune.

It is the cup of human life. We have permitted you to do little more than taste the sweet, while you have been required to drain the bitter to the dregs. Let this remind you that the wise and just man enjoys the pleasures of life in moderation, and is not ostentatious of the good that he enjoys, since by that ostentation he would insult misfortune: and that as suffering enters more largely into the lot of most men than happiness and enjoyment, we should be patiently resigned to suffer when our Father in Heaven sends us calamities and afflictions. We should be unworthy to share the benefits which society and association afford, if we were not also ready to share the evils which our Brethren and fellows suffer. Woe unto him who despairs, when he has to drain the cup of suffering to the bottom! He is unworthy to be called a man! Wherefore, if, unfortunately, thou becomest a victim, consult thy conscience! If it accuse thee, humble thyself, without abjectness, and reform! If, on the contrary, it do not denounce thee, lift up thy forehead! For God has made thee in His image and likeness; and let reflection enable thee to draw strength from weakness. Fall not in the struggle like a coward, but resist like a hero!

··

A.

From the earliest times, the Initiate into the Mysteries was subjected to physical trials of his courage and endurance. Pythagoras imposed on his disciples five years of silence. Wherever the Mysteries were practiced, and under whatever name, the good faith, devotion, and manhood of the candidate were tested, and complete assurance of them had, before he was irradiated by the Light of Truth. In the middle ages, when the Church of Rome, sit- ting on the ruins of the fallen empire, reigned supreme over consciences, Masonry, claiming as its patron Saint John the Evangelist, and thus indicating that same anti- Papal spirit which, at a later day, produced the seemingly absurd mysticism, the apparent jargon of nonsense, of Alchemy and Hermeticism, the splendid diatribe of Dante, and the broad buffoonery of Rabelais — Masonry, proscribed by the Church, as it was afterward excommunicated by Pope and King together, needed to require similar tests and trials. Like the early Christian Mysteries, it was a "Secret Discipline" For, during whole centuries, a word, the least indiscretion, a gesture, was a death-warrant. The Mitre and the Crown were then in league together against man. The Inquisition, reigning over the universal conscience in the gloomy shadow of Rome and the Vatican, classed Masons with Jews and Heretics, and dealt with them by the tender mercies of torture. Then, the populace did not flock into the Masonic Temples, and buy the Degrees with so many shekels, as a means of safety and protection. To be a Mason then, was to expose one's-self to the same dangers as surrounded, like tigers and serpents, the Christian under Nero and Domitian. The existence of the entire Masonic body was involved in every initiation.

—Masonry comes more directly from the Mysteries of the Sun, and those of Mithra, in Persia. There the aspirant commenced by easy tests, and arrived by degrees at those that were most cruel, in which his life was often endangered. No one can be initiated, says Suidas, until after he has proven, by the most terrible trials, that he possesses a manly soul, exempt from the sway of every passion, and, as it were, impassible. Gregory Nazianzen terms the tests, 'tortures,' and mystic 'punishments' and although the trials of the Eleusinian initiations were not so terrible, they were still very severe. Masonry has softened, but has not chosen to dispense with, the ancient tests; for it is not in free countries only that she exists; nor is it in them that she plays the most important part Neither, even in these, is there any guarantee of the eternity of freedom, or that the powers of government may not be usurped by Demagogue or Soldier, to whom Masonry might become dangerous, and would be hostile, unless false to its mission.

Our tests are symbolic, and not terrible or dangerous. Still, they will try your firmness and resolution. They foreshadow what you may have to endure, or violate your obligation as a Mason; and they remind you anew that your resolution must not falter, nor you purchase liberty or life by dishonor, even if, like our Masonic fathers, you should someday find yourself in the cruel and pitiless embrace of a political or religious Inquisition, that imprisons, and, in the depths of its dungeons, or on its scaffolds, immolates those who defend Freedom or teach her holy doctrines. The Inquisition never found a coward or in- former among Masons. It only sleeps, and may awake again. The Kings imitate each other. You may not always live in a country where the incontrovertible rights of human nature are respected. If they now are so in your own, you may unexpectedly see an usurper declare his will to be the only law, and be suddenly required, at any hazard, to assert the rights of the people and the majesty of the laws against him. The nation that is free to-day, may be enslaved to- morrow; the too free soonest submitting, subservient to the despot's ancient plea, Necessity. Republic yesterday, Kingdom to-day, Empire to-morrow:—such are the fantastic scene-shiftings of Nations. Therefore reflect well, before you further commit yourself! When you shall have taken a step further in advance, it will be too late to draw back. Your destiny will then have been determined.

••

THE AIR.

••

The second element is the Air, which, with its meteors, miasms, lightnings, and continual fluctuations, incessantly menaces us with death. It was anciently considered one of the means by which the souls of the dead were purified. "As physical bodies," the old sages said, "are exalted from earth to water, from water to air, from air to fire, so the Man may rise into the

Hero, the Hero into the God. In the course of nature, the soul, to recover its lost estate, must pass through a series of trials and migrations. The scene of those trials is the grand Sanctuary of Initiation, the Universe ; their primary agents are the elements, and Dionusos is official Arbiter of the Mysteries, Guide of the Soul, the Sun, the Liberator of the elements, Creator of the world, Guardian, Liberator, and Saviour of the Soul, ushered into the world amidst lightning and thunder."

Again, the air is a symbol of vitality, or life. When Yehuah-Alohim, says the ancient Hebrew cosmogony, had formed man of the dust of the ground, He breathed into his nostrils the breath of life, and man became a living soul. The air, to the Hebrews, symbolized Nephesch, or Vitality, the lowest portion of the immaterial part of man, of the trinity of Life, Spirit, and Mind. The air, therefore, is a natural and apt emblem of human life, with its cross- currents, its agitations, its stagnations, its lassitudes and energies, its storms and calms, its electrical disturbances and equilibria. So, also, the comparison of the life of man to a journey, has always been familiar to moralists and philosophers; and thus the journey you have taken is a fit emblem of that life, with its tumult of the passions, its shocks of conflicting interests, its difficult undertakings, its successes and reverses, its obstacles, multiplying and co-operating to hinder and embarrass.

But this is too trite an interpretation, though true, to be the only one. Your journey also represents the progress of a people; that progress to assist in which is the highest aim of Freemasonry. Progress is the mode of man. The general life of the human race is called progress. It is the collective advance of the human race. Progress marches; it makes the great human and terrestrial journey toward the Celestial and the Divine, from the Square to the Compasses. It meets delays, recoils at and overcomes its obstacles; it has its halts, where it rallies the belated flock; it has its stations, where it meditates, in sight of some Canaan, suddenly unveiling its horizon. It has its nights, when it sleeps; and it is one of the bitter anxieties of the thinker, to see the shadow upon the human soul, and in the darkness to feel progress asleep without being able to waken it.

But he who despairs is wrong. Progress infallibly awakens; and even in sleep it advances, for it has grown. When we see it standing again, we find it taller. To be always peaceful, belongs to progress no more than to the air and the river. Each of these meets obstructions; the air-currents flow against and around forests and mountains; the river flows over rocks. These make the air roll and eddy in billows, the water foam, and Humanity seethe. Hence storms, hurricanes, cataracts, eddies, and counter- currents, troubles, confusions, and revolutions: but after these we find that ground has been gained. The Inquisition imprisons Galileo, but the sun still moves. Until order, which is but universal peace, be established, until harmony and unity reign, progress will have revolutions for stations.

The nations, moreover, are blind, and the Destiny that leads them onward is symbolized by your guide, the Terrible Brother. Statesmen are but puppets in the hands of Destiny and Providence;

blind instruments of a Higher and Inscrutable Will. The ends to which their labors and their virtues or villainies tend, are not those for which they struggle, and toward which they seem to themselves to make the nation march. The few intellects that really and truly foresee, rarely control and govern. They are Cassandra, whose prophecies are wholly unheeded. The individual man, also, is blind, led by the cords of destiny, in the hands of those who educate him, and of the circumstances that surround him. The opinions of the mass of men are imposed upon them, not adopted upon reflection and examination. Custom and prejudice are the blind guides of the blind. Yet the truth dreads nothing; and he who does not exercise his reason, even in matters of faith, re- mains a child, a blind traveler, all his life. To forbid one the use of his reason, and to require him to accept his faith at the dictates of another, is an absurdity; since, if faith be unreasoning, no man can show in what respect his faith deserves the preference over that of another. Every man has a right to say, for himself like Tertullian, that he will believe a thing because it is a folly; and hold it certain, because it is impossible; but no man has a right to demand that any other man shall, at his dictation, do the same.

Wherefore, as you have now experienced the helplessness and abdication of manhood which is involved in being blinded and led by a guide, let no one hereafter lead you, blinded, in matters of faith; but in all things see for yourself, and judge for yourself by the laws of reason and analogy.

Finally, as after the storm comes a calm, and after the earthquake, repose; so, when the period of tests and trials shall have passed, the age of error and doubt, the tranquility of reason will be enjoyed, of that peace of the soul which satisfies the conscience. After the revolutions of progress, the stability and repose of free institutions. After the storms and conflicts of the individual life, the serenity and quiet of the soul, result of a just equilibrium of the appetites, the passions, the moral energies, and the intellectual powers. To attain this within himself, to aid his country in its progress toward it, is to do the true work of a Mason, and requires, above all things, constancy and courage.

··

THE WATER.

··

The brazen laver represents those placed by King Solomon in the Temple, and that brazen sea in the Temple, which, supported on twelve oxen that looked to the cardinal points of the Compass, was an image of the great ocean that washes the shores of the world. [B.] In the Druidical Mysteries, among the trials of the Candidate, he was placed in a boat and sent out to sea alone, having to rely on his own skill and presence of mind to reach the opposite shore in safety. This dangerous voyage, upon the actual open Northern Sea, in a small boat, covered with a skin, on the evening of the 29th of April, was the last trial and closing scene of the initiation. If the Candidate declined it, he was dismissed with contempt If he made it and succeeded, he was termed "thrice-born," was eligible to all the dignities of the State, and received complete instruction in the philosophical and religious doctrines of the Druids.

When the aspirant was to be initiated into the Mysteries of Isis, he was conducted to the nearest baths, and after having bathed, the priest first solicited forgiveness for him of the gods, and then sprinkled him all over with the clearest and purest water, and conducted him back to the Temple. It was required of every initiate that his heart and hands should be free of every stain. It was rep- resented that, except for the gravest sins, there was opportunity for expiation; and the tests of air, water, and fire were represented, by means of which, during the march of many years, the soul could be purified, and rise toward the ethereal regions; the ascent being more or less tedious and laborious, according as each soul was more or less clogged by the gross impediments of its sins and vices. In the Mithriac Mysteries, the Candidate was purified with water and fire, and went through seven stages of initiation. Ablutions were required in all the Mysteries, symbolical of the purity necessary to enable the soul to escape from its bondage in matter.

Sacred baths and preparatory baptisms were used, lustrations, immersions, lustral sprinklings, and purifications of every kind. At Athens, the aspirants bathed in the Ilissus, which thence became a sacred river; and before entering the Temple of Eleusis, all were required to wash their hands in a vase of lustral water, placed near the entrance. Apuleius bathed seven times in the sea, symbolical of the seven spheres through which the soul must reascend; and the Hindus must bathe in the sacred river Ganges. Menander speaks of a purification by sprinkling three times with salt and water. Water nourishes and purifies; and the urn from which it flowed was thought worthy to be a symbol of the Deity, as of the Osiris-Canobus, who with living water irrigated the soil of Egypt; and also an emblem of Hope, that should cheer the dwellings of the dead. In the terrible and dangerous tests of some of the old Mysteries, the Candidate was made to swim a river.

In all, the symbol of washing or baptism by water meant the same thing—purification of the hands and heart. As such it was used by the Essenes and John the Baptist, and adopted as part of the ceremonial of Christianity. It was peculiarly expressive in the hot dry Orient, where rivers are blessings flowing from God, and springs in the desert are called diamonds. Naturally, to the dweller on the Nile, the Ganges, the Euphrates, or the Jordan, purification of the body by water became the symbol of purification of the soul.

The Ocean, also, has always been an apt symbol of the People, to whose service every true Mason devotes himself. Inert in calm, and in the tropics almost stagnant, it is agitated and wrinkled by the least movement over it of the winged winds. Tortured by tempest, its huge waves shake its iron-bound shores. Its great icebergs drift through it, like empires on the seas of time. Its instability and fury picture the fickle humors and merciless revenges of an exasperated people. Its great currents are like those of popular opinion. The huge tidal waves, undulating in a few moments across the expanse of the wide Atlantic, are like the impulses that flash mysteriously through an awakened nation; and individual men are but the drops of the vast ocean of humanity, of which the nations are the waves. As the mariner must incur the hazards of shipwreck and engulfment in the waves, so must the patriot who would serve the people do so at the risk of becoming odious to it, and being crushed by it in its blind rage. Let this remind you that you must have a higher motive for your public action than office and honors; since, if the desire for these alone actuates you, you will infallibly cease to serve the people when it the most needs your services, and when to be its benefactor is most noble, because it is most dangerous and least profitable

••

••

"I indeed," said John the Baptist, "baptize you with water unto repentance; but he that cometh after me shall baptize you with the Holy Spirit and with fire."

Human ceremonies are indeed but imperfect symbols; and the alternate baptisms in fire and water, intended to purify us unto immortality, are even in this world interrupted at the moment of their anticipated completion. Life is a mirror which reflects only to deceive, a tissue perpetually interrupted and broken, an um forever fed, yet never full.

Of this purification, that by Fire was a symbol. This symbol afterwards became, in the worship of the gods, the actual sacrifice of innocents in the flames. The Hebrews, originally one people with the Phoenicians and with the Moabites, Edomites, Amunites, and other people of Canaan, thus, at an early day, as their books show, sacrificed their first-bom, and those who still spoke the same language with them, still so sacrificed to Malak (or Moloch), the King, long after the Hebrews had abandoned the practice. So it is that the symbol, especially in religions, always tends to usurp the place of that which it symbolizes; the idol comes to be worshiped as the God of which it was originally only the symbol; and the ceremony and formulas all things to a true

Man and Mason. Even the wild Indian, condemned to die, and permitted to go to a distance upon his promise to return, presents himself at the day to be slain, rather than save his life by violating his word. The soldier risks his life daily, not for his pay of a shilling, but for his duty to the flag under which he serves. Shall the Mason's love of life weigh more heavily in the scale against duty and honor than that of the rude soldier or ruder barbarian?

It reminds you also of the bloodshed in all ages by Intolerance and Persecution, and pledges you to Toleration and the defence of the sacred rights of Conscience. It reminds you of the martyrs of all creeds, dying for their faith; of the bloody sacrifices of the Hebrew altar and the Mexican Teocalli; of the stake and the rack of the Inquisition, and the gallows stretching its arm over the Christian pulpit; of all the long roll of atrocities and murders sanctioned by religion and deemed grateful service to a God of Love.

The time has come, Sir, for you to perform a simpler and easier act of Masonic duty. We have unfortunate Masons, widows, and orphans, to whom the Lodge gives continual assistance. I shall send a Brother to you, to whom you will make known in a whisper how much you are now willing to contribute for the relief of these unfortunates. You will not say it aloud; for you are to know that the charitable acts of Masons, not being acts of ostentation and vanity, to minister to the pride of him who gives and humiliate him who receives, ought always to be shrouded in secrecy. ' When thou doest alms, let not thy left hand know what thy right hand doeth; that thine alms may be in secret; and thy Father, which seeth in secret, will reward thee openly.'

━━

☉∴ Charity ceases to be a virtue, when it prevents the performance of more sacred and more pressing duties.

Civil engagements to be met, a family to maintain, relations dealt harshly with by fortune to relieve, children to rear and educate,—these create the foremost duties that Nature imposes on us; these are the Creditors of every man whose conduct is regulated by the principles of Equity. The maxim of the Law is the maxim of Masonry—'Nemo liberalis nisi liberatus.' No one must be liberal until liberated of these paramount duties. To give what is elsewhere pledged and owing, is to give what is not our own—is to give, without their consent, what belongs to others. Give, therefore, only what you can give, and yet fully perform these sacred duties! At the same time, consider not your own ease, indulgence, comfort, or luxury as creditors to be preferred to the poor. To give only so much as we could throw away without losing a comfort or mortifying an appetite, or denying ourselves the indulgence of a wish or whim, is an act of no merit, since it costs us nothing and deprives us of nothing. He who gives shillings to the poor, and squanders pounds in luxuries or gaming, may indeed do good, but there is no merit or charity in the act. Determine now what thou wilt give the destitute wards of the Lodge, out of what is thine own!

■■

.... Though the needy whom your gift will relieve, will not know from whom it comes, you will none the less be enriched by their gratitude, and benefited by their prayers.

■■

If what you have offered to give, be all that your paramount obligations will permit, and if to give it deprives you of some luxury or comfort, and truly makes you poorer than before, it is the Widow's Mite, as acceptable in the sight of Heaven as the rich man's costly offerings would the desert Country near the Jordan, clad in the garments of a penitent, and living on the food of a Bedouin, boldly rebuked the ambitious, haughty, and self-righteous Pharisees, and the skeptical and scoffing Sadducees, as a race of vipers, and preached human equality and the ultimate triumph of Good over Evil, in the Salvation of the Lord. He inculcated repentance and reformation, a liberal charity and a virtuous life. He exhorted public officers to exact no more from the people than that which the law required; and the soldiery to do violence to no one, accuse no one falsely, and be content with their legal power and pay. He sternly re- proved Herod for his sinful connection with the wife of his brother. The lewd and revengeful woman sought his death, but Herod imprisoned him without trial, and so kept him confined, until her daughter, dancing before him, his Lords and Captains, on his birthday, obtained his promise that he would grant her whatever she might ask; and prompted by her mother, she demanded the head of the eloquent Essenian Missionary.

The abuses of arbitrary power in all ages are summed up in this single legend; the baleful influences of the mistresses of Kings and Emperors; imprisonment, without trial, by lettres de cachet, and other inventions of tyranny, for acts or words that were not offenses defined and punishable by any law; the dependence of liberty and life on the mood, revengeful or lascivious, of an amorous Tyrant or wanton woman. In the arbitrary imprisonment of John we see the very essence of tyranny and despotism, the power to imprison without trial, for what is no crime defined by law; the absence or impotence of any impartial judicial power, to set free the prisoner illegally detained. In the execution, we see Murder, as committed in all ages and countries, by Kings and the Usurpers of Civil and Military power: and in John, the bold rebuker of the vices of the people, of the arrogance, hypocrisy, ambition, and infidelity of the Priest- hood, of the unjust exactions of the agents of Power or the Law, the license, violence, usurpation, and rapine of the soldiery, and the vices of the Crown and Court, we have the type of the true and genuine Free Mason, successor of the Ancient Essenes. Him you are to imitate; even, if necessary, in his fate.

■■

let him now and always be sure, that should he prove a traitor to us, there will be no comer of the wide earth, in which he can take refuge, into which he will not bear with him the stigma of his crime; that everywhere the report of his excommunication will have preceded him, as if borne by the lightning, and that everywhere he will find Masons informed of his guilt, and detesting his perjury.

■■

אור.

■■

The fortunate day of loyal friendship and living Brotherhood dawns for thee; and hereafter thou art to see in us not merely friends, but Brethren, ready with thousands upon thousands over the whole surface of the earth, to hasten to thy assistance against any who may assail thy life or honor; though thou art as yet only an Apprentice, and not entitled to the wages of a Craftsman.

On being brought to light, you see before you the Book of the Law, the Compasses, and the Square, upon the Altar of Masonry These are deemed indispensable in every Lodge, and they are called the Three Great Lights of the Lodge. You see them by the blaze of the three lesser Lights of the Lodge, on the East, West, and South of the Altar, symbols, it is ordinarily said, of the Sun, the Moon, and the Master of the Lodge. These latter are termed, also, the Sublime Lights in Masonry. The Holy Bible, it is said by our Brethren of the English or York Rite, is the rule and law of Government of Masons: the Square governs our actions; and the Compasses keep us within just bounds as to all men, and more particularly toward our Brethren.

The same Brethren say: The Bible points out the path that leads to happiness, and is dedicated to God. The Square teaches to regulate our conduct by the principles of morality and virtue, and is dedicated to the Master ; and the Compasses teach us to limit our desires in every station, and are dedicated to the Craft The Bible is dedicated to the service of God, because it is the inestimable gift of God to man; the Square to the Master, because it is the proper Masonic emblem of his office, and it is constantly to remind him of the duty he owes to the Lodge over which he is appointed to preside ; and the Compasses to the Craft, because by a due attention to their use, they are taught to regulate their desires, and keep their passions within due bounds.

And as to the Lesser Lights, they say that they are thus explained: As the Sun governs the world by day, and the Moon rules it by night, so ought the Master to rule and govern his Lodge with equal regularity.

■■■

☉∴ To the Glory of the Grand Architect of the Universe, and under the Auspices of the Supreme Council, etc.

■■■

■■■

■■■

This apron, of white lamb-skin, is the distinctive badge of a Mason; and our brethren of the York Bite say that it is more ancient than the Golden Fleece or Roman Eagle, more honorable than the Star and Garter, or any other decoration. It is at least ancient It is honorable, because it is an emblem of labor. You ought, the same Brethren say, to wear it with pleasure to yourself, and honor to the fraternity. It has, in all ages, been deemed an emblem of innocence; he, therefore, they say, who wears the lamb- skin, as a badge of Masonry, is continually reminded of that purity of life and conduct which is so essentially necessary to his gaining admission into the Celestial Lodge above, where the Supreme Architect of the Universe presides.

The apron is the evidence of your right to sit among us, and you must never be present in any Lodge without it. Its peculiar and real symbolism will be made known to you hereafter. You have already the surface- symbolism, that of the horn-book—Innocence and Candor. 'We speak wisdom among them that are perfect; not the wisdom of this world or of the Princes of this world that come to nought: But we speak God's Wisdom in a mystery —the Hidden, which God had an idea before the Universe existed, to be our Glory, and which none of the Princes of this world knew.' Paul, like the York Bite, spoke to the Corinthians as infants, having an animal and no spiritual nature, and fed them with milk and not with meat—the points of the Compasses under the Square.

∙∙∙

⊙∴ The white gloves also are part of the clothing of a Mason. Be it your care to keep them unsullied, never staining them by vice. Let your hands and heart be always pure and undefiled. Walk as a child of Light, and have no fellowship with the unfruitful works of darkness.

∙∙∙

⊙∴ These gloves the Lodge presents to your wife, or to her, who, beloved by you, may hereafter become such. They will be a fit symbol of the purity of true affection, and will be to her as a pledge on the part of the Lodge, that if she should ever need its assistance, consolation, or encouragement, an advocate or a defender, she will find all in the Lodge or among the brethren.

∙∙∙

העלמים.

∙∙∙

Masonry, my Brother, is known all over the world. It is divided into many Bites, the three principal of which are the York, or English Bite, worked in Great Britain, her Colonies, the United States, and most of Germany, and some other parts of Europe; the Ancient and Accepted Scottish Bite, and the Rit Moderne, or French Bite. Essentially, the three Blue Degrees are the same in all, though there are great differences in the work. There are differences in the language of these Bites, which you are entitled to know

∙∙∙

The tools or implements with which an Entered Apprentice works, are the Twenty-four-inch Rule, or Gauge, and Common Gavel.

'The Twenty-four-inch Gauge,' our Brethren of the York Bite say, 'is an instrument used by operative Masons to measure and lay out their work; but Free and Accepted Masons make use of it for the more noble and glorious purpose of dividing their time. It being divided into twenty-four equal parts, is emblematical of the twenty-four hours of the day, which we are taught to divide into three equal parts ; whereby are found eight hours for the service of God, and a worthy distressed Brother ; eight for their usual vocations, and eight for refreshment and sleep.'

This was Saint Augustine's division of time; and it was perhaps real with him, he being a Bishop. But there is not, nor ever was any such division of his time by one Ma- son in ten thousand; nor is it required of a Mason. Wherefore the explanation and application are faulty and incorrect. It is neither appropriate nor philosophical.

The same brethren say of the Gavel: 'It is an implement made use of by operative Masons to break off the comers of rough stones, the better to fit them for the builder's use; but Free and Accepted Masons are taught to make use of it for the more noble and glorious purpose of divesting their hearts and consciences of the vices and superfluities of life; thereby fitting their bodies as living stones, for that spiritual building, that house not made with hands, eternal in the Heavens.'

We can as little approve this application and attempt at symbolism; because the comparison is strained and artificial; the vices and superfluities of life are not divested as with a stone-hammer, and by the knocking off of rough corners.

When those who made our Association what it now is, concealed its true nature by adopting the name and character of a particular body of Artificers, in order that they might pursue their great and beneficent purposes in safety, they, of course, adopted the implements of that trade, and distributed them among the different classes of their members. To the Entered Apprentices they assigned those of the appropriate hard and rudimental labor, the hammering or cutting down to certain lines and dimensions the rude rough blocks of stone. Probably these implements had originally no symbolic meaning. It is true, that in the hieroglyphic language of Egypt, a hatchet denoted God, and a cubit, Justice. But it is not to be imagined that the Rule and Gavel were adopted as symbols of Justice and God, because something resembling each was a symbol in Egypt, any more than that the Gavel alludes to the hammer of the Norseman's God, Thor.

The Rule is a natural symbol of accuracy in workmanship; of strict definition and limitation; of Statutes and Law, of rigid, unbending Justice. The Hammer, or Gavel, is an emblem of Force, and therefore of Labor, which applies Force to Matter. The peculiar Masonic use of this Force, and that accurate regard to the lines defined and marked, is to shape the double-cube, or symbol of perfection, out of the rough Ashlar, or block of stone. If Masonry were merely an association for the moral improvement of our individual selves, and if a Mason had no more to do than to hammer off 'the vices and superfluities of his own heart and conscience,' some exclusively moral application of these implements might be admitted. But it is by no means so. There never was any need of association, secrecy, and terrible obligations, for that.

The Gavel symbolizes Force: the Force of Numbers, of Intellect, of Passion, Energy, Enthusiasm; the Force of Truth, Right, and Justice ; the Force of the Principles of Freedom, Equality, and

Brotherhood; the immense Force of Ideas; the Force combining all these Forces; of the Order of Free Masons, and of a People resolved to be free.

In the printed volume of the Morals and Dogma of the Symbolic Degrees, which you must carefully study before you can advance, you will find a full explanation of what we understand to be symbolized by the Rule and the Gavel. To that volume you will hereafter be frequently referred, and it will perhaps furnish you, as it is intended to do, with food for sober, serious, and profound reflection.

▪▪

You are taught in Masonry by Symbols. These were the almost universal language of the ancient theologies. They were the most obvious method of instruction; for, like Nature herself, they addressed the understanding through the eye; and the most ancient expressions, denoting communication of religious knowledge, signify ocular exhibition. These lessons were the riddles of the Sphynx. 'The Gods themselves,' it was said, 'disclose their intentions to the wise, but to fools their teaching is unintelligible.' The King of the Delphic Oracle was said not to declare, nor, on the other hand, to conceal, but to intimate or signify. The Mysteries were a series of Symbols; and symbolical instruction is recommended by the constant and uniform usage of Antiquity. The mysterious knowledge of the Druids was embodied in signs and symbols; and Taliesin, describing his initiation, says 'The Secrets were imparted to me by the old Giantess' (Ceridwen, the same as Isis), 'without the use of audible language. I am a silent proficient.'

The method of indirect suggestion, by allegory or symbol, is a more efficacious instrument of instruction than plain, didactic language; since we are habitually indifferent to that which is acquired without effort. 'The Initiated are few; though many bear the Thyrsus.'

Symbols were used to a great extent, to conceal particular Truths from all except a favored few, who had the key to their meaning. To the mass of the Initiated, only some trite and obvious explanation was given, the primary among many readings. The meaning of the Symbols of Masonry is not unfolded at once. We give you hints only, in general. You must study out the recondite and mysterious meaning for yourself. A single symbol often has several meanings. There are, indeed, to almost every one of the ancient among these Symbols, four distinct meanings —one, as it were, within the other;—the moral, political, philosophical, and spiritual. The Apprentice and Fellow-Craft are taught only the two first.

The Symbols of these degrees are partly Ancient and partly Modern. The Ancient have come down to us from the old Mysteries, of which we have already spoken; but of which we shall not treat in this degree.

The first scene, in the Greater Mysteries of Eleusis, was in the Outer Court of the inclosure, as this place, where you have been received, signifies the outer Court or ground-floor, the Pronaos, of King Solomon's Temple. The Candidates were awed with terrific sights and sounds, while they painfully groped their way as in the gloomy cavern of the Soul's sublunary migration. For by the immutable law, exemplified in the trials of Psuche, man must pass through the terrors of the under-world, as you have done in the dungeon and cave, before he can reach the height of Heaven. The material horrors of Tartarus, as depicted by Virgil, were represented to the Candidate. Successive scenes of darkness and light passed before his eyes, and many mystic representations of wondrous magnitude and beauty.

Astonishment and terror took his soul captive : in the Mysteries of Isis, he passed through the dark valley of the shadow of Death, and then into a place representing the elements, where the two Principles, Darkness and Light, symbols of good and evil, clashed and contended. In the Dionysiac Mysteries, the Candidate was kept in darkness and terror, three days and three nights. If you thought that we kept you too long blindfolded, learn that in this also Masonry has softened down the tests of the Ancient Mysteries! In the Mysteries of Eleusis, there were frightful scenes, alternations of fear and joy, darkness and light, glittering lightning and the crash of thunder, the apparition of specters', or magical illusions, impressing at once the eyes and ears.

There are Catechisms in this degree, called in the York Rite, 'Lectures which you must learn. To commit them to memory is indispensable. The first repeats the mode of your initiation, step by step: the second gives the explanation of and reasons for that ceremonial: the third describes the Lodge and its furniture, and gives the primary meaning of these as symbols.

'Masons,' our French Brethren say, 'build Temples to the Virtues, and dig dungeons for the vices.'

The Donjon or Dungeon is a Symbol of Royal and Feudal Power; of the rule of the Inquisition, the Monastery and the Cloister. There are dungeons for Nations also, in which these sit and crouch, and shiver and decay into their dotage , loaded with gyves, fetters, and manacles; the bones of their good and brave flung into the corners, that they may weep bitter tears over them; Liberty lying in her Coffin; the Skeleton of their old glories against the wall; the lamp of Superstition, instead of the Sunlight of Truth and Reason, enabling them to read the sad record of their woes and shame ; the bread and water of the prisoner, fit diet for the laggards and lurdans too easily taken in the net; the skull, holding the sepulchral lamp, teaching them that their feeble light will soon be quenched in darkness, and they go down to join the old dead Despotisms. Slaves to the dogmas of Divine Bight, of time-honored authority, legitimacy, and sacred tradition, the Salt, the Sulphur, and the Mercury fail to remind them that Nations, like individuals, have not only bodies, of the earth, earthy; but Souls, that should respond to the calls and inspirations of Honor and Pride, and to the sentiments of Liberty, Equality, and Fraternity; and Spirits, that should irradiate the world with the light of Philosophy, Thought, and Intellect.

And, before we pass finally from the Dungeon and the Cave, let us return to the first and simplest lesson they teach. A perpetual remembrance of the tomb is proper for the living. All must die. To mingle with our life a certain presence of the sepulchre, is not only the law of the ascetic, but of the wise man. In this relation, they tend toward a common centre.

・・・

The Candidate in Masonry is in Search of Light. He represents both an individual man and a People. As one and the other, he comes from the darkness and he wanders in the darkness, until, first guided by the Terrible Brother, Experience, in which are involved Suffering, Calamity, and Distress, and afterward by Reason, as the Master of Ceremonies, Faith and Love, the two Deacons, unseal his eyes to the Light of Knowledge and Liberty. The darkness and the Preparation represent the condition of the Individual, slave and prey of Ignorance, Superstition and Tyranny, of Error and Vice: of the People, at once the blind instrument and bound victim of Power that oppresses, Craft that enslaves, and Policy that brutalizes. He is emphatically a Profane, enveloped in mental darkness, poor and destitute of rights and knowledge. He holds even what he earns by the frail and uncertain tenure of the will and pleasure of his Tyrants and Masters: and round his neck is the threefold cord of servitude and bondage, to Royalty, the Church, and the Nobility.

・・・

Nakedness and bare feet were symbols, with the Hebrews, of degradation, subjugation, affliction, humility, and sorrow. He has already 'eaten the bread of adversity, and drunken the waters of affliction.' Tho heart is on the left side; and to 'bare ' it, is symbolically to open the heart, by which are denoted frankness, and entire absence of fraud, deceit and concealment The heart, to the Ancients, was the seat of the passions, emotions, and affections; and although its functions are now well known, the word is still used by all men in the same metaphorical sense.

To 'bow the knee,' is an expression used to indicate an act of worship and adoration. 'Abrech!' 'Bow the knee! 'was cried before Joseph, when, after he had interpreted Pharaoh's dream, that

Monarch freed him from prison, made him his Prime Minister, arrayed him like a Prince, and caused him to ride in triumph in his second chariot 'I will leave seven thousand in Israel, all the knees which have not bowed unto Baal;' said the Lord to the Prophet Elijah. 'Strengthen ye the weak hands, and make strong the feeble knees! Say to them that are of a fearful heart, be strong; fear not!' says the Prophet Isaiah. The right side of the body, and the limbs on that side, are symbolical of Strength. It is the right hand of the Lord 'that doeth valiantly and is exacted, that is become glorious in power, in the Psalms: when Jacob blessed Ephraim and Manasseh, he laid his right hand, as the superior in blessing, on the head of Ephraim the younger, though Joseph remonstrated; because the younger was to become greater than the elder, and his seed a multitude of Nations. 'From His right hand went a flame of Law for them:' said Moses, blessing the children of Israel before his death.

Every Masonic Lodge is styled a Temple; and you have been made a Mason in a room and place representing the outer Court [אוּלָם Aulam or Avalam, 'ο πρόναος, Vestibulum, porticus] of King Solomon's Temple. Among all the Oriental nations, the Priests and others were required to be barefooted, on entering holy places. 'Put off thy shoes from off thy feet!' said the Angel of the Lord, in a flame of fire out of the midst of a bush, to Moses: for the place whereon thou standest is holy ground! '—'Loose thy shoe from off thy foot! 'said the Prince of the Lord's Host to Joshua, for the place whereon thou standest is holy!' When David fled from Jerusalem, upon the rebellion of Absalom, 'he went up by the ascent of Olivet, and wept as he went up, and had his head covered, and he went barefoot' 'Go!' said the Lord, by Isaiah, ' and loose the sackcloth from off thy loins, and put off thy shoe from thy foot!' And he did so, walking naked and barefoot, three years, for a sign and wonder upon Egypt and Ethiopia, and a premonition of their captivity to Assyria. 'Forbear to cry! Make no mourning for the dead! Bind the tire of thy head upon thee, and put on the shoes upon thy feet!' said the Lord, by the mouth of Ezekiel, to the Jews.

In Ancient Egypt, the Hierophant, sacrificing to the Sun, first laid aside every ornament of a metallic nature.

The young Brahman, when inducted into 'The order of a twice-born man,' was invested with the sacred cord, of three threads, so twisted as to make three times three, and called Zennaar and Yajnoparita. It was an emblem of the Deity, three in one, Brahma, Vishnu, and Siva, Creator, Preserver, and Destroyer. Hence the Cable-tow. But this Cable-tow has to Masons a peculiar and significant symbolical meaning, concealed in its name, which seems to be merely an antiquated English word.

....

You were told what that was to teach you: but it was also to teach you that those among whom you desired to enroll yourself were men, knowing their rights, and possessed of arms to defend them; and that they were prepared to meet with the symbol of Loyalty and Honor, the emissaries of Tyranny, the spies or mercenary soldiery of Power. This portion of the ceremony comes to us from the Mysteries of Mithra, in Persia, where the Candidate, entering the Cavern of Initiation after his novitiate, was received in the same manner. A people, rising in its majesty to assert its rights, must be baptized in blood.

In the Indian Mysteries, as the Candidate made his three Circuits, he paused each time he reached the South, and said, 'I copy the example of the Sun, and follow his beneficent course.' Daily the Sun rises in the East, journeys by the South and sets in the West: and yearly, leaving the Equator at the Autumnal Equinox, he falls more and more to the South, on the ecliptic, until, at the Winter Solstice, the Feast of St John the Evangelist, he reaches the Tropic of Capricorn. There, seeming to pause for three days, he again gradually ascends, crosses the Equator at the Vernal Equinox, continues northward, and pauses at the Tropic of Cancer at the Summer Solstice, the Feast of St John the Baptist

In the Druidical Mysteries, the Candidate was conducted nine times around the Sanctuary, from East to West Your attention will be continually directed to the number 3 and its combinations. With perhaps a few hints, it will be left to yourself to fathom the meaning of that part of our symbolism.

We have already spoken at large of the symbolism of your purifications. Engrave upon the tablets of your heart these solemn words of the Prophet Isaiah:

"Wash you! Make you dean! Put away the evil of your doings from before mine eyes! Cease to do evil! Learn to do well! Follow Justice! Relieve the oppressed! Defend the fatherless and see them righted! Plead for the widow! "

Your three purifications also allude to Ezekiel's description of that out of which came the likeness of the four mystic creatures of his vision and of the Apocalypse, each having four faces,—the face of a Man and the face of a Lion, on the right side; the face of an Ox and the face of an Eagle on the left side; each with four wings, and the hands of a man under their wings on their four sides. These creatures of flame, over whom was the Throne of God, and who flashed to and fro like lightning, came out of the midst of a whirlwind from the North, a great cloud, and a fire infolding itself: and thus the three elements, the air of the whirlwind, the water of the cloud, and the fire, are mysteriously connected with the four symbolic animals. Study for yourself the hidden meaning. And, in the meantime, remember, that Nations, like men, to be free must first be virtuous. For them, too, the purification of fire and blood. 'When the Lord shall have washed away all the filth of the daughter of Zion, and shall have purged Jerusalem of the blood shed therein, by the spirit of justice and the efficacy of fire,' only then can she possess the holiness of Freedom. On the lips of the Nations also must the Seraphim lay the live coals from the Altar of God, that their iniquity may be taken away and their sin purged.

You have taken upon yourself an obligation of secrecy, in the antique form, as solemn as those taken by the ancient Initiates. The crime of violating it would deserve, if it did not receive, the fearful punishment which the old laws imposed.

In the Island of Crete, Jupiter Ammon, or the Sun in the Zodiacal Constellation of the Kam (in which Constellation the Sun then was at the Vernal Equinox), had a tomb and a religious Initiation; one of the principal ceremonies of which consisted in clothing the Initiate with the skin of a white lamb. This is the origin of our Apron of white lambskin. The apron itself is modern; adopted when the Order concealed itself under the mask of a handicraft, and took as symbols the working-tools of Stone-Masonry. It is not only a symbol to us of Labor and Work, but of Purity and Innocence; and to all Christian Masons, of their faith in 'the Lamb of God that taketh away the Sins of the World;' a figure and symbol taken from the old Hebrew ceremonial, according to which either seven or twice seven lambs were sacrificed on each of the ten days of the Seventh Month, on which solemn Convocations were held; while on each only a single goat or kid was sacrificed as a sin-offering; the latter being peculiarly sacred to the Principle of Evil, and sent, loaded with the sins of the People, to Azazel, in the desert. The whole symbolic character of the Apron is lost, when a piece of cot- ton or linen is substituted for the lamb-skin.

As a symbol of expiation, it must continually teach you that it is your duty and privilege as a Mason, to sacrifice yourself, if need be, for the welfare of the Order or of your Country. So to become, in some sort, the Redeemer of a People, is the highest glory and loftiest honor of Humanity, and connects the Human Nature with the Divine. To build up in Men's minds the idea of Progress; to forge those liberating dogmas which are Swords by the pillows of the Generations; to work and to suffer with the People, —even, if need be, to the extreme of sacrifice ; is the destiny and duty which a true Mason accepts.

Our Lodges are, or should be, situated due East and *West; because, our English Brethren say, all Temples are so situated; and these were so, because the Gospel was first preached in the East, and afterward extended into the West Another reason, they say, is, that the Tabernacle of Moses was builded east and west, and that Solomon, in imitation of it, so builded the Temple.

The Tabernacle was a movable oblong tent; but when-ever set up, it was probably placed with its mouth to the rising Sun; since the North, South, West, and East sides are spoken of in its description and the description of its Court. The Temple, like the Pyramids, was built by the Cardinal points; and Ezekiel saw in his vision the Glory of the God of Israel coming from the way of the East, and entering into the House by the way of the Gate toward the East. It was an oblong square, 60 cubits long, by 20 wide, the Oracle or Holy of Holies at the West end, 20 cubits square; the Inner Court, 40 cubits by 20; with a porch the whole width of the building and 10 cubits deep, in which was a wide gateway.

The three Sublime Lights of the Lodge are, the Sun or Osiris; the Moon or Isis; and Horus, Hermes, or Khorom, the Master of Light, Life, and the Universe. This leads you to the threshold of all the mysterious doctrines of the old philosophies, to the gates of the Kabalah, the Veda and Zend-Avesta. It is not yet time for you to enter in, or to know the meaning of the equilateral and right-angled triangles, of the tesserated pavement in alternate lozenges of black and white; of the number three so constantly presented to you, in the threefold cord around your neck, the three raps at the door, the three circuits, the three columns of the Lodge, the three greater and three lesser lights, the three Officers of the Lodge and its three jewels movable and three immovable, the three purifications, the three articles of furniture, the three ornaments, and above all the three triangles interlaced, white, red and green. You must study, my Brother, be patient, and wait.

Yet we shall not entirely refuse to enlighten you, by hints which if you are an apt disciple of the Sages, you may understand. Meanwhile we again refer you to the Volume of Morals and Dogma.

••

You will find in the Volume of Morals and Dogma all that is to be made known to an Apprentice in regard to the Symbolism of the Plumb, the Level, and the Square. Of the Ashlars we have already spoken there; and we only add, as a hint to induce reflection and persuade to study, that the Oraculum or Holy of Holies, the Kadosh Kadoshim, or inner apartment of the Temple at Jerusalem, was a perfect cube, twenty cubits square, and the same from floor to ceiling.

The Tracing or Trestle-Board is an oblong Square on which designs are drawn, by the Master Workman, for the government of those under him, in the erection of edifices. It is therefore a symbol of Instruction, Education and Law; and thus has both a moral and a political meaning. The Master of the Lodge represents Wisdom or Reason; and the Trestle-Board teaches us, morally, that our conduct should always be regulated in accordance with the dictates of Sound Reason, and not by Passion or Impulse. Every man being a rational being, should have a plan of life and conduct, and should steadily pursue it, following always the Compass of Reason, and not permitting the winds of circumstance to blow him from his course.

And, although in a Free State the Law must be the expression of the will of the People, yet it should be, not the utterance of its follies, ignorance or passion, but of its wisdom. The power of making the laws should be committed to the wisest, to the men of knowledge, and the men of intellect. Then there will be harmony, consistency, stability and permanency in the laws. And the Trestle-Board is an apt symbol of those Free Constitutions, solemnly adopted by the general will, irrevocable and unalterable except in accordance with their own provisions, which are intended to survive the shocks of time, to guarantee private rights and an equitable exercise of the Powers of Government, to make usurpation of tyrannical authority impossible, whether in peace or war, and to be the resplendent Ægises of Liberty, the Great Charters of Human Right

••

The head of the Column of the North is the place which you will occupy in this degree. There laboring assiduously and studying zealously, you may earn the right, in due time, to be admitted to the more secret and higher mysteries, and to receive those favors which the Lodge never denies to those who prove themselves worthy.

••

⊙∴ I do proclaim and I do accordingly require all the Brethren to recognize him for the future as such, and to give him aid and assistance whenever he may by the cement of Brotherhood. As an Apprentice you are to build up this moral Temple in your own heart: and to aid in erecting the Universal Temple of Liberty upon the Earth. It is the Mason who erects fortifications: and in a free Country, Free-Masons are to build them against the enemies of Freedom, against Error, Intolerance and Usurpation, Luxury and Corruption, Fraud and Ambition.

The ancient Poets, in their allegories, said, that Neptune and Apollo offered themselves as masons to Laomedon, to help him hold the walls of Troy. They meant that these gods dictated to him the Laws and eternal principles of Truth, and of Civilization sustained by Material Force.

In the confident belief that you will prove yourself a good and faithful Craftsman, the Lodge which receives you into its bosom, is now about, according to the ancient form, to applaud your initiation, and to salute and congratulate you by

••

.... See how feeble, and liable to error, is Human Nature, when we follow our impulses and instincts, without sufficiently reflecting on what we are about to do.... Always remembering how you were about, in the very presence of the Altar, to err and fall, be merciful to error in others.
••

ADDRESS OF THE ORATOR.

ADDRESS TO VISITORS.

My Brethren, the bond which unites us, and makes of all the Masons in the world one living Soul, has brought you here to assist us in our labors. We accept this as an assurance that you will also toil with us beyond the doors of the Lodge, in the great labors which belong to Masonry. Whether Catholics, Protestants, Israelites, Mohammedans, Sabæists, believers or doubters, we meet here to build up, by united effort, the Altar of Toleration in the Temple of Freedom, because we all follow the Law of Love, which is the efficient principle of morality. For us the odious distinctions of the Profane World, dividing it into parties and nationalities, have no existence. We are Brethren: Worshipers at the same Shrine. The spirit of Provincialism disappears before the unity of Idea; and personal interest sacrifices itself to the general interest of universal civilization and happiness. Receive the sincere expression of our thanks for the favor you have done us; and permit us to salute you by the mysterious Numbers of the Degree!

ANOTHER.

My Brethren, in the name of all the toilers in the great and sublime work of the regeneration of man, and especially in behalf of the Brethren of this Lodge, I thank you for coming to our assistance and encouraging us by your presence, to-night. A little knowledge of human nature teaches us that such visits, especially of the learned and eminent, are great incitements to emulation and the attainment of excellence, and almost indispensable to prevent assemblies of Masons from sinking by degrees and almost without a struggle, into the quicksand's of discouragement and apathy; into the dull, cold, heavy repetition of formulas, to that condition of the Church in Laodicea, when their works are neither cold nor hot, but lukewarm; when they think themselves rich and increased with goods, and in need of nothing, and do not know that they are spiritually wretched and miserable and poor and blind and naked, occupied only with the dead formulas of the ceremonial.

Continue, my dear Brethren, to assist and encourage us, and invite us to assist and encourage each other. Men easily become faint-hearted, and are as easily encouraged and elated; so that with little cost to himself, of trouble or exertion, one may, by his mere presence, work much good, inciting his brethren to works and service and charity and faith and patient hopefulness, which is Strength. Let us not forget, my Brethren, either within the Lodge or without, that the word 'Charity' does not mean the giving of alms, but Affection and Loving-Kindness; nor how often a word of sympathy, kindness and encouragement saves the wounded, distressed, discouraged, doubting Soul from total disbelief in the goodness of God, from sinking in the leaden waves of despair and crime; the man from becoming a drunkard and a criminal; the woman from plunging into the sewers of Vice; and both from self-abandonment, ruin and pollution.

Grateful for your presence, the Lodge will be still more thankful for any words of counsel and good cheer. Meanwhile, permit it to salute you by the mysterious Numbers of the degree, after the ancient custom

⊙∴ The Poor ye have always with you.

⊙∴ Let us do good unto all men, especially unto them that are of the Household of the Faith! According as everyone hath received the gift, so minister the same one to another, as good Stewards of the manifold favors of God! Charge them that are rich in worldly wealth, that they do good, that they be rich in good works, ready to distribute, willing to share their wealth with others, laying up in store for themselves a good foundation against the time to come, that they may lay hold on eternal life!

THE FUGITIVE LEAVES.

PRAYER.

Grand Architect of the Universe! Immortal and Inexhaustible Source of Light and Life! The Workmen of this Temple give Thee a thousand thanks, ascribing to Thee whatever that is good, useful, or glorious there may be in the works of this day, and thanking Thee for a new addition to their numbers and strength. Continue, we pray Thee, to protect them! Guide them onward in the way that leads toward Perfection! And let Harmony, Peace and Concord ever cement their work! Let Friendship and good works ever adorn this Temple and here dwell and inhabit! Let Generosity, Loving Kindness and Courtesy always characterize the Brethren of the Lodge! And in the outer world help them to show by their words and conduct that they are true Children of the Light! Amen.

TABLE- OR BANQUET- LODGE.

ARRANGEMENT OF THE LODGE.

The hall in which the banquet is held, should be so situated that no one without can see or overhear anything.

The Table is to be, as nearly as possible, in the shape of a horseshoe. The Master sits on the outside, at the summit: the Wardens at the two extremities.

The Orator is at the head of the Column of the South, and the Secretary at that of the Column of the North. The East is occupied by Visitors, or by the Officers of the Lodge if there are no Visitors.

No other Officers than those named have any fixed place. If there are Visitors of the higher degrees, who fill the East, then the other Visitors will be at the heads of the Columns.

When all are seated, the Venerable will use his pleasure in regard to the first Health; whether to give it before eating anything, or after the soup, or at some other period.

When he wishes to give the first health, he raps once with his Mallet. If there are Serving brothers, they withdraw immediately from the interior of the horseshoe, and retire to the West. So they do at each health. All cease to eat. Ordinarily the Bro∴ Master of Ceremonies is alone within the horseshoe, fronting the Venerable, to be better at hand to receive his orders and see them executed. Sometimes he sits at a small table between the two Wardens.

FIRST HEALTH.

☉∴ Brethren Senior and Junior Wardens, be pleased to announce upon your Columns that the first obligatory Health is that of 'The President and the Congress of the United States!' We will add to this Health our wishes for the success of the arms of the Nation in War, and its honor and prosperity in Peace. It is a Health so dear to us, that I invite you to deliver your fire as handsomely as possible. I claim for myself the words of Command.

SECOND HEALTH.

☉∴ Brethren Senior and Junior Wardens, the second obligatory Health, which I have the honor to propose, is that of 'The Governor and Legislature of the State of America'

We will add to this Health our wishes for its continued Sovereignty, Independence and Freedom; and that it may ever vindicate its honor, assert its authority, and protect its Citizens against Usurpation. The Health is so dear to us, that I invite you to deliver your fire as handsomely as possible.

••

THIRD HEALTH.

This is given according to the same formula. It is: 'The Judicial Departments and Officers of the United States, and of the State of A' We will add to this Health our wishes that the Independence of the Judicial Power may be always maintained, that it may never be op- pressed by the Military Power: and that its capacity to protect the property, liberty and life of the Citizen, may never be diminished.

••

FOURTH HEALTH.

This is prepared for as before. It is: * The Most Puissant Supreme Council of Sovereign Grand Inspectors-General of the 33d degree, for, whose See is at.' We will add to this Health our wishes for the prosperity of the Masonic Order in general Be pleased to invite the Brethren of each Column to join me in delivering the most Masonic and fraternal fire.

••

FIFTH HEALTH.

Given as above, is that of 'The Grand Consistory of Sub- lime Princes of the Royal Secret, of the 32d degree of the Ancient and Accepted Scottish Rite, for the State of A' — if there be a Consistory in the State in which the Lodge is holden.

••

SIXTH HEALTH.

Given as above: 'The Most Worshipful Grand Lodge and Grand Master of Ancient, Free and Accepted Masons of the State of
A" We will add to this Health our fraternal wishes for its Health, Prosperity and Continuance, and that of the Brethren who constitute its Masonic People.

■■

SEVENTH HEALTH.

☉∴The Health which the Brother Junior Warden, the Brother Orator, and myself have the honor to propose, is that of the Venerable Master who directs the labors of, this Lodge, and of all who are near and dear to him. Be pleased to join us in delivering the best possible fire.

■■

EIGHTH HEALTH.

The Brethren Senior and Junior Wardens.

■■

NINTH HEALTH.

This is: 'The Visiting Brethren who honor us with their presence.' To this we will add the Health of all Lodges affiliated or corresponding with ours.—Union! Contentment! Wisdom!

■■

TENTH HEALTH.

This is 'The Officers and Members of the Lodge!' To this we will add the health of the Brethren recently initiated.

LAST HEALTH.

☉∴ ♩♩♩. Brethren, Senior and Junior Wardens, the last obligatory Health is that of all Masons spread over the whole surface of the Earth, whether in prosperity or adversity. Let us with reverence invoke for all the favor of the Grand Architect of the Universe! That it may please Him to succor the unfortunate and bring them into good harbors! Be pleased to invite the brethren on your columns to unite with us in delivering for this Health the most efficient of fires.

PARTING SONG OF MASONS.

1. A-dieu! a heart-fond, warm a-dieu! Dear Brethren of the Mys-tic Tie!
Ye fa-vored, ye en-lightened few, Whose secrets Gold nor Pow'r can buy:
Tho' far a-part our paths may lie, Still to our ob-li-ga-tion true;
With melt-ing heart and brim-ful eye, You'll think of me, and I of you.

II∴ Oft have we met, a social band,

And spent the cheerful festive night; Obedient to our Chiefs command,

The Sons of Honor and of Light And by that Hieroglyphic bright,

Which none but Craftsmen ever knew, Shall Memory on each true heart write, — 'You'll think of me, and I of you! '

III∴ May Freedom, Harmony and Love Unite us in the grand design, Beneath the Omniscient Eye above, The Glorious Architect Divine!— May we still keep the unerring Line, Act by the Plumb in all we do, Answer the summons and the sign!— You think of me, and I of you!

IV. Honor to all whose right and claim To wear our sacred badge is clear;

And triple honors to each Name To Scottish Masons justly dear!

We part, perhaps no more to hear

In the same Lodge words wise and true; But through what stormy seas we steer, You'll think of me, and I of you!

....

CLOSING- SONG.

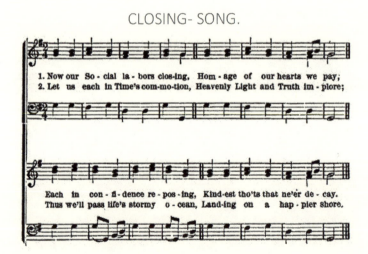

Soon we part, the word once spoken, Friend from friend in kindness goes, Thus, till Time's last ties are broken, Be the claim each brother knows.

On the Level meeting, ever By the Plumb act, just and true, Part upon the Square, and never Fail *good work* and *square* to do.

··

☉∴ Our labors are closed. Let us retire in peace!

··

מדרגה שנית.

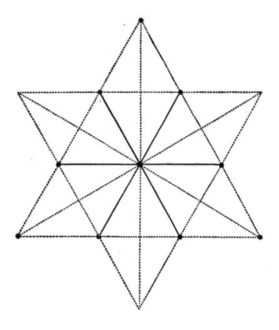

Second Degree

II.

FELLOW-CRAFT—COMPAGNON.

TO OPEN.

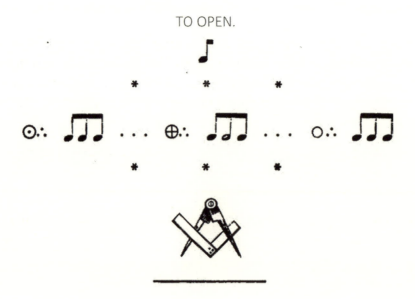

PRELIMINARIES OF RECEPTION.

When it is proposed to pass an Apprentice to the degree of Fellow-Craft, the following provisions are to govern.

An Apprentice cannot be passed until he has served his time, that is, has been present at five meetings of his Lodge, for instruction. He ought to be twenty-three years of age; but this the Grand Master or Inspector General may dispense with, if he is over twenty-one.

When it thus becomes permissible, the App∴ will apply for the Second Degree, making his application specially to O, on whose Column and under whose inspection he will have worked.

• •

The Lodge may postpone the proposition to another day, if there is not time to discuss the matter fully, or if further information is desired. If it is not proposed to postpone, ☿ will conclude for passing or delay. Then the ballot will be taken, as to his conclusions, in the manner directed in the Apprentice's degree.

It requires a vote of two-thirds of the Brethren present, to permit the Candidate to pass. . . .

• •

All the brethren of the Lodge must be summoned to attend the meeting at which the Candidate is to be passed; and the Summons should inform them that there will be a reception in the Second Degree, so that any who could not attend the previous meeting, may be present at this, and object, if they have any good cause. The Summons to an Apprentice will not mention any work at which he cannot assist.

On the day of reception all the brethren will be admitted to the Lodge. The Lodge of Apprentices will be opened, and after reading and approval of the record of the previous meeting, the Master will direct the Apprentices to retire.

But if there be no work to be done in the Apprentices' Lodge, nor any banquet, the Apprentices need not be summoned. In that case, the record of the Apprentices' Lodge will remain unread, until a meeting of that Lodge, when all are present.

••

RECEPTION.

••

A short time only has elapsed since you were initiated an Entered-Apprentice Mason. If found qualified, you may now advance, having attended five meetings of a Lodge, for instruction. It is said that anciently five years were required to elapse, which was the time during which those who attached themselves to some Sects of Philosophy were required to study.

The Degree of Fellow-craft is Fellowship, Education, and Science. Like the Apprentice's Degree, it deals exclusively with the moral and political meanings of the Symbols, except so far as the Philosophical and Spiritual necessarily mingle with and interpenetrate Morality and Political Science.

Before you can proceed, we must know that you have made due proficiency in the preceding Degree. To under- stand the instruction of this, that of the former must have been understood and must be constantly kept in mind. If you have not taken the trouble of engraving that in your memory, and on the tablets of your heart, or if you are not capable of doing it, self-respect would forbid our casting any further instruction before you. We shall therefore proceed to examine you in regard to the symbolic meaning of the points of your entrance, and of the Lodge and its details.

••

EXAMINATION.

⊙∴ You are now about to make progress in Masonry. The Fellow-craft's degree is Progress. It teaches Brotherhood, Education, and Science. In them and in Moral Improvement, true Progress for the Individual or the Nation consists. If you would realize what Progress is, call it Tomorrow. Tomorrow performs its work irresistibly, and it performs it to-day. It always reaches its aim through unexpected means. It ever goes on, not always steadily, but more often fitfully. It is a Workman to whom no tool comes amiss. It adjusts its divine work to the man who strode over the Alps, and the feeblest tottering invalid. It makes use of the Cripple, as well as the Conqueror, of the Knave as well as the Saint

The delay required to elapse, after you were initiated, before you could be permitted to receive the Second Degree, was intended to give you the needful time in which to prepare yourself, by imprinting on your memory, so that its characters should remain indelible, the instruction of the First Degree, to fit you to make progress in the Second. In the Ancient Mysteries, that interval was of several years. Thus the Egyptian Priests tried Pythagoras, before admitting him to know the Secrets of the Sacred Science. He succeeded, by the patience and courage with which he surmounted all obstacles, in obtaining admission to their Society, and receiving their lessons. In Palestine the Essenes admitted none among them, until they had passed the tests of several degrees.

In this Degree the five years of study required by............................. Pythagoras are symbolically represented by................................. At the end of each you will receive the appropriate instruction.

The Rule or Twenty-four-inch Gauge is one of the Working-tools of an Apprentice. Its meaning was explained to you in that degree. Keep it in mind in this! Disorder is the law of Weakness. Let the Rule still be to you the Symbol of Law, Order, Intellect, controlling and regulating Force. Rule, in the Latin, regula, is Government, restraint, the limitation and management of Force. But remember, also, that it is **MOTION** which gives *method*, on the Earth, as in the Skies,—that *reveals* **POWER,** as among the electrical elements. Movement is the result of an alternating preponderance. The scales of the Balance must alternately rise and fall. Immobility would be stagnation and death.

א

MUSIC.

The Chisel, used by means of the force of the Mallet, serves the Workman for smoothing and polishing with constant and intelligent labor the materials for his creations. It is, above all, the chief tool of the Sculptor, with which he cuts away the envelope that in the rough block of marble conceals and hides the Statue; and by which he develops the Gladiator, Symbol of Strength, and the Jupiter of the Capitol, Symbol of Majesty, or the Venus, Symbol of Beauty.

The Apprentice, working with the Gavel, employed force alone, cutting down the Stone to certain straight lines, marked by the unbending inflexible Rule, under the directions of the Master. The Sculptor, using the Chisel, uses it with judgment, and with judgment applies the force of the Mallet, whether he carves the beautiful and delicate vase, in accordance with the lines of beauty, creating the graceful wreath and exquisite foliage, or invests the Statue with the poetry of his art. Even the Stone-cutter, shaping the Cube, the oblong Stone, or the Column, and more especially the Corinthian or Composite Capitals, must exercise his skill and judgment in the use of the Chisel.

The Morality of the Line and Rule is not sufficient for the Fellow-craft. These will give Honesty, Uprightness, Truthfulness, Punctuality, and Puritanism. The work of the Chisel is wanting, or the character is hard, dry, and ungenial. It is perfected by those genial virtues and fine graces which are not dictated by the stern rules of law, or the Ten Commandments ; by Generosity, Liberality, Courtesy, Amiability, Gentleness, the soft relentings of forgiveness, by all the graces and beauties, which are as the flutings and capital of the Column, the curves, the flowers and foliage of the Vase.

In the Apprentice's degree, as in a lower school, are symbolized exact discipline, and the training of the faculties for future use. In this, as in an upper school, you must train Thought, that it may at once be wedded with healthy Act.

■ ■

Love the Truth! Abhor the Untruth!—that is the first requisite. Without that, you can neither improve yourself, nor serve the People. Let the Mallet and Chisel first rid you of all duplicity, dissimulation, equivocation, and dishonesty. Until then you are not a man, and circumstances may make you a villain.

■ ■

To secure moral and intellectual freedom to an individual, or political freedom to a Nation, is a work of Thought, Patience and Perseverance. It is a work that goes on by slow steps ; and the harder the toil with which a People hews the steps out of the solid rock, the surer is the final ascent. If there is any earnest work on earth, it is where the road to Freedom is being paved. The Tree of Liberty must come up ou the spot, from the seed, and not be transported bodily, in bulky growth. The Thought must explain the trials of the time; but the march in the desert gives the discipline, and Temperance will give the triumph.

■ ■

Thought, the noblest characteristic of the isolated man, is also that of a People. Our purpose now is, to teach you to think. Men may become wise without many books. It is true that he is fortunate who has the leisure to study, and add to his knowledge. The Fellow-craft ought, it possible, to obtain a knowledge of the Natural Sciences. The more he knows of the Universe, the better he knows its Author. And these Sciences, especially Geology, necessarily lead the Student to think and reflect. But the intelligent man may attain great results by Thought alone. Free men are serious. They have objects at their heart, worthy to engross attention. It is reserved for slaves to indulge in groans at one moment, and to laugh at another.

Our ancient instruction says, is a Symbol of the term of one year, which a Fellow-craft was required to pass in perfecting himself in the work of cutting and smoothing the Stones, which as Apprentice you learned how to rough-hew. This Work, with the Chisel and Mallet, is to teach you, that the degree of perfection which an Apprentice can attain, is far from finishing his work; that the materials consecrated to the building of the Temple which he rears to the Grand Architect, and of which he is at once the material and the Workman, are not yet ready for the building; and that he must still undergo the hard and toilsome labor of the Mallet, and learn, accurately and with precision, to use the Chisel, never varying from the lines traced for him by the Masters. You must interpret and apply this for yourself.

••

MUSIC.

••

It is said that during the second year of the studies of the Disciples of Pythagoras, they studied Geometry, to which Arithmetic is the introduction. In the theory and practice of Geometry, the Compasses and Rule or Scale are indispensable; and that is one reason why you have borne them in your journey.

The Compasses, also, are the Symbol of the Circles which it describes, and of the Celestial Spheres. In conjunction with the Rule, it represents the Divine element, intermingling with the laws of Morality and the rules of Political science, by which alone perfection, symbolized by the Cubical Stone, can be attained, or even approached unto.

A man may strictly comply with every positive obligation imposed on him by the law, and even with all contained in the moral code, and yet be detestable. A community of men, in which each should punctiliously observe the law and that code, would be one in which no generous soul could live. If the divine, in morals, did not intermingle with the human, the world would be intolerable.

••

The Compasses, also, by which round a fixed point we describe the Circle, emblem of Deity or the Supreme Wisdom, are themselves an emblem of that Wisdom. With their aid, too, upon the base laid down by the Rule, we erect the equilateral triangle, Symbol of many things, and, to a Fellow-craft, especially of Liberty, Fraternity, and Equality.

••

This signifies Preparation,—the study of Principles, which fits a Fellow-craft to do the Work,—whether by the Fellow-craft is meant an individual or a people. The practical elements must be acquired, before they can be applied. The elements of Mathematics must be thoroughly understood, and its problems demonstrated, by the aid of the figures traced by the Compasses and Scale, before they can be applied in Surveying, or the measurement of land; in Navigation, or that of courses and distances on the pathless ocean ; in Coast-Surveying, which marks the shoals and reefs that cause shipwreck, and with the aid of the Compass, of his reckonings and observations, and of the logarithmic tables, enables the Mariner, in the darkness of night, and amid the terrors of the frightful storm, to find safe harbor; or in Astronomy, which measures the distances, orbits, specific gravity, and mass of the Planets, and enabled Leverrier to ascertain, before his telescope discovered it, that another Planet existed, by the measured perturbations of its neighbors .

To all this, Science attains, by the use of those simple instruments, the Compasses and Scale. The Line and the Circle are the great elements of Mathematics. Of these, the Scale and Compasses are the Symbols. From Moral Rectitude, and the Wisdom that teaches Love and Faith, results the perfection of the individual man, the interpenetration of the human by the Divine; and from Justice and Wisdom results good government in the State

For the Rule is the Symbol, naturally, of direction and control,—of rule, regularity, inflexible or unbending Principles. Reguloe Juris, the rules of Law, do not shift and vary with the fluctuating tides of circumstance, nor disappear in the presence of Necessity or Expediency. These are only for to-day. Principles are for all time, the same yesterday, to-day, and to-morrow; as the Deity is all that was, is, and is to be. To-morrow, Necessity and Expediency will have disappeared like the mists of Morning; the Principles will remain and shine with undimmed lustre, like the Stars

The Fellow-craft is, in pursuing his studies, to lay up principles for future use. Remember, that, in all cases, the use of a doctrine, and the only reason for its being promulgated and accepted, is its translation into action. Even the sublime doctrine of Christ is of no great use to the every- day violators of it, how bitterly soever they may hate all dissenters from its truth.

• •

....

ג
MUSIC.

During the third year of the studies of the Disciples of Pythagoras, it is said in our old Rituals, an Apprentice is taught bow to move and place in position the Stones for the foundation of the building, which is done with the aid of the Rule and the Crow or Lever. The Lever, it is also said in the same, is the Symbol of the power of Knowledge, which, adding to our individual strength, enables us to do and effect that which, without its aid, it would be impossible for us to accomplish.

" Behold, I lay in Zion for a foundation, a Stone, a tried Stone, a precious corner-stone, a sure foundation; he that believeth shall not be too hasty. Judgment also will I lay to the line, and righteousness to the plumb."

"The God of Jacob," it is said in Genesis, "is the Stone of Israel."

"The Stone which the Builders rejected, is become the head of the corner."

" Ye are no more strangers and foreigners," Paul says to the Ephesian Christians, " but fellow-Citizens with the Saints, and of the Household of God; and are built upon the foundation of the Apostles and Prophets, Jesus Christ himself being the Chief Corner-Stone, in whom all the building, fitly framed together, groweth into a holy Temple in the Lord."

You are now to commence the erection of that Temple of Virtue, Morality, and Freedom of the Mind and Soul, which is symbolized by the Temple of Solomon. That edifice was erected by Solomon on Mount Moriah, where before was the threshing-floor of Oman or Araunah the Jebusite, purchased by David.

'The King commanded, and they brought great

Stones, costly Stones, and hewed Stones, to lay the foundation of the House. And Solomon's builders, and Khurum's builders did hew them, and the Stone-Squarers,' or men of Byblos,—the Giblemites.

The length of the House was sixty cubits, or one hundred and two and a half feet; and its breadth twenty cubits, or thirty-four feet. There was also a porch, or portico, ten cubits, or seventeen feet wide, along the whole eastern front: making the foundation an oblong square, measuring nearly 120 feet by 34. Solomon's own house was much larger, being, with the porch, 221 feet long, by 85 wide.

It is the uses for which the .Temple was intended, that make it symbolical. It was for the public worship of the Deity; and in the Oracle, Holy of Holies or Kadosh Kadoshim, the western room, the Shekinah or Divine Presence was supposed to dwell between the Cherubim.

To the Fellow-craft, as you already know, the Temple symbolizes an Individual and a State. The foundation of the moral or political Temple is to be laid by the help of the symbolic Lever, to the lines laid down by the Rule: and it is to be laid of great, costly, hewn symbolic Stones, like the Cyclopean work of the Etruscan Architects, yet to be seen in the ancient foundations of Rome. The foundation-stones of the Temple still remain, some of them twenty- four feet in length by four in width, beveled in the edges, of a very white limestone resembling marble, and forming, when cemented together, a perfectly solid wall or foundation, which only a convulsion of the solid earth could demolish.

Thus firm, solid, stable, and durable should be the foundation of the character which makes the Man, of the knowledge which makes the Scholar or the Statesman, of the State that is to endure. Courage, resolution, decision, firmness , persistence, endurance, hopefulness, self-respect, self- reliance, the chief ingredients of manliness; forethought, temperance, fortitude, hardihood, energy, justice, rectitude, fairness, loving-kindness, faith and faithfulness, devotedness and disinterestedness,—these are the chief of the great, costly, hewn Stones of the foundation of an admirable character. Classical learning, the natural and physical sciences, the Law of Nations, the Laws of Trade, knowledge of the great commercial currents and financial phenomena, and familiarity with great Constitutional principles, are those of the foundation of the learning of the Statesman. The Great Principles embodied in Charters of the public Liberties, in Bills of Eight, and written or unwritten Constitutions, are those of the foundations of a Free State

• •

Let the Fellow-craft, therefore, and even the humblest Apprentice be encouraged to work, not apprehensive, in whatever direction he may work, that his labor will be lost. No Force, nor any action of any Force, is lost, in this universe. There are no blows struck in the void. Paul, after his conversion, was not a person of much consideration, and the sphere of his labors was the preaching of a new and unpopular faith, anti-idolatry in an idolatrous world, He wrote a few letters, all of them together not as long as a single modern Speech of some windy Boanerges,—

letters to handfuls of obscure individuals in the great Empire City, Rome, and the great Provincial Cities of Corinth and Ephesus, and in some Roman Provinces, and to the obscure persons, Timotheus, Titus and Philemon: and what a wonderful work in the world those letters have wrought! What, by the side of them, or of Luther's Sermons even, are Moscow-expeditions and Waterloo's? The great works of the world are done unexpectedly, like the invention of printing, by obscure men. Let us all take courage, therefore, and work!

••

ז

MUSIC.

During the fourth year of the service of an Apprentice, our ancient Rituals say, he is employed in the erection of the body of the edifice, and in accurately placing in position the Stones of which it is built; and it teaches you, it is there said, that only application, zeal and intelligence can raise a Fellow-craft above the general level of his fellows.

A Throne, whether of King or Free People, should stand on the golden backs of strong lions, bound by the wisdom of the circling serpents, and canopied by the silver doves of Mercy. But Wisdom cannot be entailed. The lust of idleness is a disease that preys alike on People, Peers and Princes. History proves that the sense and right of public duty cannot secure exertion. Families perpetually wear out, by the un- willingness of Nature to propagate the useless plants.

••

The Masonry of the Ancient and Accepted Scottish Kite, based on the foundations of Morality and Manliness, is, first of all, hostility to Tyranny. It is the Apostolate of Liberty, Fraternity and Equality

---

A free people may speak its mind with fullness; but after decision it must obey, as well as the serf. Respect for the Law should be greater in Free States than in those that have Masters, and where public opinion has not cut and deepened the great channels. For it is the law made by themselves for themselves. Reverence for the law is self-reverence. For Officers, Civil or Military, who violate it, and usurp power, and crush Constitutional guarantees, the mandates of the Law should be concise and stern, like those of the Twelve Tables.

When usurpation is once in the saddle, it is not easily unseated. The title ripens by prescription; and if the people become a little used to it, only the most intolerable outrages will rouse them to annihilate the new-born Despotism. Always remember that you entered here by the right of being free-born; and therefore oppose the very beginnings of tyranny.

Law distinguishes the criteria of Eight and Wrong; teaches to establish the one, and to prevent, redress or punish the other; employs in its theory the noblest faculties of the Soul, and exerts in its practice the cardinal virtues of the heart. It is a Science, universal in its use and extent, accommodated to each individual, yet comprehending the whole Community. It is or ought to be the perfection of human reason, the expression of experience and wisdom, gathered from the whole human family, and applied to the wants of Communities. It is founded first on the study of the universal human nature; and that study is a Science in itself. It is a moral as well as a practical Science. Law is Morality in office. It is progressive as man himself, following him with equal steps. It is a heroic work to amend the law.

Simplicity and not show, honest administration and not corruption, the silent rule of the law, and not the glittering and noisy empire of arms, are characteristics of free Government. Kings parade their power before the people in the midst of armed men, and their reviews are as much meant for their subjects as for the enemy. A free Country is not meant for spectacle. They that rule themselves are conscious of their strength, and simplicity becomes splendor. The People grants or revokes the commissions of its Generals, the patents of power of its Rulers. The allegiance of the willing hearts is beyond that of the bayonets. Conscious strength is silent. The National acts would hardly be known, but for the press. Mankind may not be better than of old:

there may be the same old love of lucre, the same lust for power, the same hunger for patronage. But the People act and speak through the Press, sit in perpetual oversight of men and the things they do, and drag to light the deeds that delight in darkness. Through it they tell those in power that they are not immortal, and that their power is but a brief trust. If there be trafficking in forbidden wares, the vail is drawn aside at last in the open market. In the end, all things are tested by the Square and Rule.

The old Romans gave official nobility. They allowed a man to bear the surname of Africanus, Capitolinus or Coriolanus, and thus linked a noble name to a noble deed, — a possession and an example forever. This privilege inspired the family more than a Peerage held in heirship. True, the love of excellence is different from the love of distinction, and better. It consists in the desire to do good deeds, and it longs for the words on earth, that many will hear only in Heaven:—'Well done! Thou good and faithful servant!' But the love of distinction is natural and laudable; and distinction is valuable, when conferred on excellence alone. The badge of Honor, or the Office, which mediocrity and trickery can attain, loses its virtue in the estimation of honorable minds. A free people should take care not to cheapen its rewards. It is more fatal and more foolish than to depreciate its currency by shamelessly breaking its faith. Wages to the workman: honor to the worthy! A man were better hang himself with the Garter of Nobility, than wear it when he has not earned it. He only who has borne the Cross is worthy to wear it. Let men be bribed and bought with money, if you will, but not with place or honor. Appoint the fittest, and promote the best. Honors distributed by any other rule are dishonors. If you have a vote, you have a voice, indirectly, in the conferring of all honors; and how much or how little soever your vote may weigh, if you do not give it for the best, you to that extent undermine the foundations of the State.

Youth will naturally vote for Youth: and its knowledge is ordinarily superficial, its counsels rash and impetuous. It is apt to prefer the shallow and the sprightly, to the profound and solid. A single House of Legislators, com- posed chiefly of young men, would prefer the swift speed of impulse to the slow progress of prudence. Hence, in free Governments, the Legislature is generally divided into two bodies, a lower and more numerous, and an upper, of fewer men, and these of greater age. A free people are ever young, and have the impatient temper of Youth. Hence an appeal lies naturally to Age; from the Man to the Sage; from the hour to the year. Age sits in the seat of Posterity, and considers its judgment. In this House ought to be gathered up the golden harvest of wise experience. It should be a real 'Assembly of the Notables,' of the wise men and elders, deputed by common consent. In a free land the wise men ought to be seen as plainly as the Mountains or the Monuments. '

So, in part, with the Square and the Rule should the House of the Temple of a State be builded. Fortunate the workman, who can use well the tools!

∙∙∙

ה

··

S ... ○ .... ♫ ♪ ... P∴ W∴
W ... ⊕ .... ♫ ♪ ... P∴ W∴
E ... ♄ .... ♫ ♪ ... P∴ W∴

··

The fifth year of the studies of the disciples of Pythagoras was devoted chiefly to Astronomy and Numbers. It is said in our old Rituals, that during this year the Apprentice studied the theory of Architecture: and he was advised, it is said, that it was not sufficient for him to be well grounded in the principles of morality and virtue, but that it would require continual effort and constant self-denial to approach toward perfection.

··

The Sword is the Symbol of Loyalty and Honor.

It is the significant emblem of the Military power, as the Defender of Liberty.

··

There is a spiritual loyalty, from Thermopylae, and Curtius leaping into the gulf, to the latest noble self-sacrifice of heroism. The loyalty of man to man is such, that he will not only kill himself, but his idol, as when Virginius slew his child, and the Roman freedman killed his master to save from worse. Loyalty to kings has been common. A thousand breasts have often been bared to save the hero from the swords of thickening foes. Napoleon's dying Veterans, at

Waterloo as at Austerlitz, in direful defeat as well as in glorious victory, uttered with feeble voices their old cry of devotion. The man personified the principle. Men died for Glory, Honor and Duty. The loyalty of the Knight to his Leader and Lady; of the Jesuit to his Order and the successor of Loyola; of the Templar, the Knight of Si John of Jerusalem and the Teutonic Knight, to his Order and Grand Commander; that of the Crusaders to the Cross, were all developments of the Divine. When men ceased to reverence Kings, Loyalty became obedience to the Law, and the love of the Soldier for his Colors and Captain, and of the Sailor for his ship and flag. Thus personal loyalty was sublimated into Patriotism and the Cardinal Virtues.

It is a truth in morals that the Soul may brutalize the body, as much as the body may degrade the Soul. There is reciprocal sympathy between them. The body is not flung beneath the brazen wheels of the car of Juggernaut, until the miserable spirit of the man has already all but perished in the dust before the foul Idol. A religion of craven fear, and abortive hopes, without love, as without light and liberty, ends, like the enchantments of Circe, in transforming men into brutes. A sound and healthy and vigorous morality depends upon a healthy religious faith. To get that, is one chief object of your last year of study. We shall in time come to resemble whatever God we believe in. Theory always crystallizes into practice. A cruel God will have cruel worshippers. Man becomes the image of the God of his creed.

Every true Word is the Word of God. He is the great Fountain of Truth. All true thoughts are inspirations. The true Orator is a Prophet: the babblers are the Prophets of Baal. Speech, thoughts spoken and printed, are the great lever by which Nations are moved, the Storm-Winds that lash the great heaving popular Ocean into convulsions,— the Word of Christ, that stills the restless waves. But, unfortunately, all speech is not the utterance of true thoughts, or even of any thoughts whatever; and babble is often more available with the people, than genuine speech.

The Mason must be ever ready to defend with arms the old flag of the Order, on which are emblazoned the magical words, great always, though often misunderstood,—"LIBERTY! EQUALITY! FRATERNITY!" Among the Soldiery of this Army of Freedom, may well be that boundless ambition, which is the spur of renown. In it there is no barrier which merit cannot pass. There is an instinct in all freemen that courts the danger leading to an eminence, and makes life weigh little in the scales against Glory and Honor.

■ ■

Every Free State ought to beware, not only of wars which exhaust, but of governments which impoverish. A waste of the public wealth is the most lasting of public afflictions; and the Treasury which is drained by extravagance, must be refilled by crime.

The Apprentice is a youth who has not attained his majority. The Fellow-craft is the Citizen entitled to vote; and also entitled, if he can attain it, to office and power. If you should embark in the game of chances called Public Life, make the Square and the Rule, uprightness and fair and equal dealing, your rules of action. Cease not to be the gentleman, if you become the candidate. Offer yourself for office, and no more. Become not base in the whining beggary for votes; or baser by trickery and the sowing of slanderous lies against an opponent. Neither expect to escape slander, nor cease to be patriotic when misunderstood and reviled, when your motives have been pure. Men will see a fault in the conduct and calumniate the motives: when your conduct has been blameless, they will remember its former errors, and assert that its present goodness arises only from some sinister intention. You will be termed crafty, when you have in reality been rash; and that will be called the consistency of interest, which in reality is the inconstancy of passion. The chief business of Party is to traduce the Great and elevate the Small.

Finally, if you discover that you are wanting in foresight, be honest, cease to mislead the people, and retire to private life. Apply the same rule mercilessly to others. The man who blunders to-day, will blunder to-morrow. Near-sightedness of the Intellect does not improve by age, like that of the eyes.

■ ■

MUSIC.

....

The Degree of Fellow-craft realizes the hopes of him who desires to learn, and of him also who is wise. For in it the Secret of our Mysteries begins to be opened, and the vail which covers them to be drawn aside. And while he who as yet knows not that Secret, sees that everyone may comprehend it, the Sage is glad to find himself among his Peers.

Upon the tracing-board of this degree, you see the representation of the front of King Solomon's Temple, with a winding stairway of three, five, and seven steps. It is the great Symbol of our Order, and has more than one meaning. Whether you will learn them all, will depend upon yourself. The value of the Secret is in proportion to the intelligence and Excellency of him to whom it is intrusted. The man to whom Virtue is but a name and Liberty a chimera, will little value the light you have already received; and he to whom Philosophy is foolishness will less value that which is perhaps to be given you hereafter. The bats and the owls prefer the obscure twilight to the light of noonday. As little can the selfish and heartless value as an emblem the Chain which encircles the Temple, with its eighty-one mystic knots. They can neither appreciate the Brotherhood of an Order like ours, nor that electric chain of sympathy, which, causing the fate of every man and his conduct to be influenced and controlled by the actions and fortunes of others, makes of a people, and even of the whole human race a single individual.

The Temple is, among other things, a Symbol of Science. The man who is familiar with the mechanism of the Universe, and its phenomena, with the laws that govern the movements of the Spheres, singularly connected as they are with Numbers; with the laws of generation, growth and crystallization, with the world of vegetation, the organic revolutions of the earth in past ages, and the marvelous wonders of minute life disclosed by the microscope, will have developed his Reason and parted with the absurd notions of childhood and ignorance. The natural and physical Sciences are the great, costly, hewn Stones of the Temple of Science.

Pythagoras inscribed on the door of his Temple these words: 'He to whom Geometry is unknown, is not worthy to enter into this Sanctuary.' By Geometry, we have already said, is meant the Mathematics, or the Science of Numbers. Mathematical demonstration attains its results with unerring certainty. Numbers, to Pythagoras, were the first principles of things; and the natural laws, of the distances and orbits of the Spheres, and the forces of gravity and attraction are singularly connected with them. It has not been deemed irreverent to characterize the Deity as the Great Geometrician, as well as the Grand Architect of the Universe.

The Masonry of the York Rite applies the number five particularly to the Orders of Architecture; the Tuscan, Doric, Ionic, Corinthian and Composite: and the number seven to what were once styled the Liberal Arts and Sciences, Grammar, Rhetoric, Logic, Arithmetic, Geometry, Music and Astronomy. Five is also remarked upon as connected with the Senses. That Rite has selected the least striking illustrations or applications of these numbers; and the rudimental information it gives on these subjects may be read in any of the Monitors, and is familiar to school-boys.

The three first Steps of the Temple of individual perfection, are Faith, Hope and Loving-Kindness: the next five, number of the aggregate of the Senses and of that of the Orders of Architecture, symbolize the aggregate of the manly Virtues and moral Excellences. The seven, number of what were once called the Liberal Arts and Sciences, symbolize the aggregate of learning and intellectual acquisitions which adorns and completes the character.

In the State, the three Steps are Liberty, Equality and Fraternity : the five, the great institutions of the State, which are, the Executive Power, the Legislative Authority, the Judicial Interpretation, the Church and the Army: the seven symbolize the Arts and Sciences, fostered by and adorning the State.

The five Orders of Architecture may also be symbolic of the five principal divisions of the religions; Polytheism; the Philosophic Paganism of Athens and Alexandria, of Socrates, Plato and Hypatia; Hebraism; Christianity; and Mohammedanism; and also of the five different forms of Government; the Patriarchal; the Despotic; the Oligarchic; the Democratic, and the limited Monarchical: thus opening to the Fellow-craft a vast field of study.

The Blazing Star is the Symbol of Civilization and Enlightenment: the letter G., of the Deity, of Geometry and all the Arts and Sciences; and of Government.

● ●

Your toils as a Fellow-craft are now to begin; you have completed your work as an Apprentice.

הנדרים.

● ●

. . . To the place whence he came, and there let him be re-invested with that whereof he was divested, and return to the Lodge for further instruction.

MUSIC.

∙∙

Hereafter, my Brother, you are to labor upon the pointed Cubical Stone, or the Cube, with a Pyramid erected on one face; and you will receive your Wages at the Column Boaz. And this new work, our old Rituals say, should remind you that a Fellow-craft, whose business it is to keep the building in repair, ought to use every exertion, not only to conceal the faults of his Brethren, but by his example and counsel to lead them to reform. Always we encounter the same trivial and common-place explanations.

The Cube, with the Pyramid super-posited, is the symbol of a Free State. The Cube represents the People. The four faces of the Pyramid are the Departments to which the People commits its powers;—the Executive, Legislative and Judicial, and the Church. These unite in the single point of Unity of Will and Action.

On this you are to work. It is therefore necessary you should have working-tools. Those of a Fellow-Craft are the Square, the Level and the Plumb. The Square, you already know, is the jewel of the Master, the Plumb of the Senior Warden, and the Level of the Junior Warden. They symbolize the building squarely up, with great stones laid truly and horizontally, the perpendicular walls of the fabric of individual character, and that of the State. They are also symbols of the three great Powers of the State, on the healthy and independent action of each of which, and the performance by each of its appropriate functions, depends the continuance of the State.

The Square is a symbol of Control, and therefore of the Executive Power, vested in a hereditary or elective Chief Magistrate.

The Plumb is a symbol of Rectitude or Uprightness, of inflexible Law and Regulation, and therefore of the Legislative Power.

And the Level is a Symbol of Equality in the Sight of the law, and of impartiality; and therefore of the Judicial Power.

They are Power, Wisdom, Justice.

The law is the same for the State as for the individual: calamity shall follow as the consequence of wrong. 'He that walketh righteously and speaketh uprightly; he that despiseth the gain of oppressions; that shaketh his hands from holding of bribes, that stoppeth his ears against bloody advice, and shutteth his eyes from seeing evil: he shall dwell on high: his stronghold the impregnable rocks; bread shall be supplied him, and water not fail.'

∙∙

In the ancient English work of this degree, the Staircase consisted of eleven steps, in five divisions; the Mystic Numbers, 3, 5, 7, and 11, following each other. The number Five reminded the Candidate of 'the five remark- able points in the ever-blessed career of our Lord and Saviour Jesus Christ:' and Eleven, 'of the miraculous preservation of Joseph, who preceded his eleven Brethren into Egypt.' These are mere puerilities.

The Numbers and Stair-way are Cabalistic. In that system of Philosophy, there are ten Emanations from the Deity or Sephiroth, through which one ascends in thought to the Absolute, Nameless, Unmanifested Deity, and with these is Death, human Thought, product of the Divine Wisdom and the Human Understanding.

The Hebrews attached a numerical value to every letter. The Great Name of the Deity, which we render 'Jehovah,' was composed of four letters; three, with one repeated: Yud, He, Vav, He: and the numerical value of these letters, in the same order, was, 10, 5, 6, 5, which added together make 26. 3, 5, 7 and 11 make also 26.

XII.

The Cross is the symbol of devotedness and self-sacrifice. From the time of the Crusades, it has belonged to Fellow- craft Masons. Pointing to the four quarters of the Compass, consisting of two lines intersected at right angles by each other, so that, though infinitely prolonged, no two of the extremities could ever meet, it was honored as a striking symbol of the Universe by many Nations of Antiquity, and imitated by the Hindus and Celtic Druids in the shape of their Temples. The Crux Ansata was a Cross, with a Serpent in a Circle above it. The Tau Cross is a most ancient symbol. ' And the Lord said unto him,' says Ezekiel, 'Go through the midst of the City, through the midst of Jerusalem, and make the letter Tau upon the fore-heads of those that sigh and mourn for all the abominations that be done in the midst thereof.' The Tau was the emblem of Life and Salvation. It was set on those who were ac- quitted by the Judges, as a symbol of innocence: and the Military Commanders placed it on Soldiers who escaped unhurt from the field of battle, as a sign of their being saved by the Divine protection.

Stat Crux, dum volvitur Orbis,—the Cross stands, while the World revolves,—was the device given his Order by Martin, the eleventh General of the Carthusians. So let Free-masonry always stand, true to her ancient principles, the Champion and Tribune of the Peoples, the Advocate of the rights of Man! Whatsoever revolutions there may be in the profane world.

In your studies, you will have constant occasion to remark how extensive has been the corruption of words, how general the loss of the true meaning of the Symbols. A Rite which transmuted Pythagoras, a native of Crotona, into Peter Gower, an Englishman resident at Groton, in England, owes it to accident, if it has preserved anything accurately. Take, for example, the word Shibboleth. A Roman name of Jupiter was Lapis, a stone, or Lapidem, stony. In making bargains, the Swearer held in his hand a flint-stone, and said, ' If knowingly I deceive, so let Diespiter, saving the City and the Capitol, cast me away from all that is good, as I cast away this stone.' Whereupon he threw the stone away. Hence the origin of the term, 'Sebo lithon, I Keep the stone;' applied among our Ancient Brethren as a testimony of retaining their original vow, uninfringed, and their first faith with the Brotherhood uncorrupted.

Our old Rituals say that the Blazing Star is the emblem of that genius which soars to the loftiest heights; and the symbol of that sacred fire with which the Grand Architect of the Universe has endowed us, by the light of whose rays we must discern, love and practice Truth, Justice, and Equity.

'The Delta,' they said, 'which you behold all blazing with light, offers you two great Truths and two sublime ideas. You behold the Name of God, as the Source of all Knowledge and all Science. It is symbolically explained by Geometry. This sublime Science has for its essential basis, the profound study and infinite applications of triangles, under their veritable emblem. All these mysterious truths will develop themselves to your eyes in succession, and in proportion as you advance in our sublime Art.'

My Brother Fellow-craft, always remember that Masonry does not seek to explain its purposes, and still less to ex- pound its philosophy and dogma to those who have not entered its sanctuaries. Very properly its teachings are con- fined to the Initiated. It does not seek to make proselytes nor to preach its truths upon the highways. It needs defense, apology, and vindication or excuses as little as Religion does. We, in this Rite, do claim for Masonry that it is a Religion, for it recognizes the great religious truths of the existence of the Deity and the immortality of the soul. Upon these broad truths Religion has fixed its foundation. In enforcing these truths, we do not usurp the prerogatives of the Priest or Pontiff. Side by side at our altars the Christian, the Jew, the Brahman, the Turk, and the Parsee, can kneel and acknowledge the one God and Creator. If Morality is a part of Religion, then we teach a pure and perfect system, not taken from the books of any one Religion, but from the teachings of Confucius, Zarathustra, Buddha and the Brahmans, from the Vedas, the Zendavesta, and the Koran, as well as from Plato and Seneca, Moses, Paul, and Jesus of Nazareth. If morality is not a component part of religion, then we invade the domain of no religion by teaching it. If the knowledge of the Creator, of His designs, purposes, motives, and nature, is no part of religion, we may rightfully learn these from the Book of Nature, God's earliest revelation. His hieroglyphics are seen in every tree and shrub, in the water and on the land, in every animate and inanimate thing. Science makes men God's interpreters. The man of science deciphers His hieroglyphics; and as he comes to know and understand better those symbols, he has a larger and better knowledge of the Deity. If a true and sound philosophy as to the Deity and nature is not a part of religion, that which remains after they are taken away, constitutes a realm of thought undisturbed by us, and to which the ministers of religion are welcome.

Masonry to the Masonic Brethren is a search after, and a journeying toward Light. The Masonic Light is Truth. It is the inculcation of truth by means of symbols and instructions. Teaching a pure morality by its lessons and lectures, it is also a great system of philosophy and of political and of religious truth concealed by symbols. It is Isis, with her vail unraised, holding out to the initiated the symbols it inherits from the ancient mysteries, the same that were used by the sages of ancient India, Persia, Egypt, and Greece.

Masonry is not opposed to any religion, nor does it seek to take the place of any religious faith. It has a Creed that underlies all religions. It has always been, and is now, op- posed to persecution for opinion's sake. Through its teachings it is the Apostle of Toleration. Eminent divines of the Episcopal, the Presbyterian, the Baptist and the Catholic sects, the Rabbi, the Brahman, the Mohammedan, can kneel hand in hand at its altars, since they all believe in the one living God. Christian divines by thousands belong to our Order, not only in this land, but in other countries, all assenting not only to the moral teachings and simple doctrines of the Blue or Symbolic degrees, but to the wise doctrines of the New Law of Love taught by it elsewhere.

My Brother, every Order and Association, like every man, and every nation, has duties commensurate with its means, powers and capacities. Our Lord, Jesus of Nazareth, taught us that, by the parables of the unprofitable servant and of the wise and foolish virgins.

We are all the almoners of God, not only to dispense in charity the wealth and goods he lends us, but to use for the benefit of others, and of society, all else with which he has so richly endowed us—our influence, intellect, knowledge , all the forces of our physical and intellectual nature. Unless we are faithful to these trusts we do not ascend from the Square to the Compasses, nor advance from the High Place of Gibeon to the threshing-floor of Oman, the Jebusite. We must account to Him for all the intelligence and influence and other gifts he has so bountifully bestowed upon us. Do we use to the utmost for good the power and influence which association gives us? Do we fully appreciate what are the great forces by which the destinies of communities and nations are controlled? Every force of nature is a direct exertion of omnipotent power. The powers of Government are not the chief of these. History, for the most part, only babbles when it tells us what was done by statesmen and soldiers. The scholar who drafted Magna Charta was the Great English Legislator, and infinitely greater than King John, who merely put his name to it. Legislation and the making of statutes are but of secondary importance to the preconceived opinions of the people. Legislation can- not lead or form those opinions. The power of legislation is only a power of police and taxation. There are now nine-tenths of the statutes of our law-books that are a dead letter, being framed only for the exigencies of the occasion existing at the time when they were passed. Legislators are only the blind instruments of Providence. The Past makes laws for the present and future. It is the dead who govern, and the living obey their mandates. The Statesmen of the present age are the slaves of those who have preceded them; they are mere puppets, moved by invisible wires. The real Legislators of the world are not those who now make the law. They are the men who died centuries ago; Moses, Plato, Confucius, Zarathustra, Mohammed, Paul, and Alfred the Saxon ; those great Roman lawyers, Paulus, Gaius, Ulpianus, Papinianus, and those who, under Justinian, revised the legal code. We are making laws for the future, as those who have preceded us made laws for us. It is not done by legislative enactments, but by our every word and action. Every word we speak is either for good or evil, and, therefore, our examples should always be for good.

The Press is a power of the same kind, which controls and forms the opinions of the people.

The most potent of the moral forces are thought, the will, example and influence, sympathy and loving-kindness. A heroic thought uttered by one man even in a solitude, but written down and repeated, may never die, but finding a response in the hearts of others may become a trumpet-call to arouse the future generations and be the cause of revolutions: and no one is ignorant of the immense force of individual will.

Influence and example have in all ages exerted their power and sympathy: when Masons clasp hands, what a magnetic thrill passes from heart to heart. The power of loving-kindness is perhaps the greatest of them all. It makes the warrior as gentle as the woman, and softens the asperities of life. And then the power of growth. The small seed is planted, and remains undisturbed for a time, and you find that it has shot forth a little tender shoot, which you may nip off, if you choose, with your finger-nail. Leave it alone, to grow! Visit it again, by and by, and you shall find that the plant has forced its root to the depth of a foot or more into the ground. Can anyone tell how it grows, or what its force is? No one knows but the Almighty, who causes it to grow and flourish. Nations and Orders grow in the same way that plants do, they also having their vital force of growth.

The vast power of association is very sensibly felt in our lodge-rooms and temples; where that sympathy and loving-kindness, which are so like the sunshine and the rain, and the dew which falls upon the growing plant, should create that magnetic attraction which bind heart to heart in unity. The growth of Masonry is a necessity to its being. Let it grow, for it does some good to every Mason, and all are the voluntary or involuntary instruments of its purposes. We cannot isolate ourselves from our fellow-men who are not of our Craft. The evils of society affect us as well as others. We are all shareholders in the public morality; and our Masonry must be made to prove its titles to respect by its good influences in the world outside of our Lodges.

Masonry combines all the forces that we have enumerated. It is an association for a common object, and in its possession of these its growth must inevitably resemble and be analogous to that of nature. It has the power of thought; and thoughts that are wise and true are laws of the human race. It has the force of will, which, in a just undertaking, may be irresistible. It has the powers of ex- ample and influence. It is already felt in the farm, the market-place, in the church and the halls of legislation. It has but to avail itself of its legitimate powers and forces, to become the greatest benefactor of Humanity. If it can become the master of religious Prejudice and Intolerance, and even maintain its Sovereignty over men's hearts during the clash and conflict of Civil War, what may it not effect in the days that are to come?

It is not to be expected that our Order shall be always prosperous, nor is it desirable. Reverses must overtake it; periods of persecution, of apathy and lukewarmness must come; unvarying prosperity will be full of dangers to it, for then it will commit fatal errors. We are thus taught bravery and endurance, and never to be discouraged nor disappointed. But we are taught still other lessons; that the life of man is like the ascent of the mountain. He must slide backward, become at times faint-hearted, wander into by-paths, commit errors, have his lapses, his aberrations of mind, his hours of folly, and nights of regret. We must not judge him by these, for they are inevitable.

Let us not recount and lament with idle wailing life's ills and maladies, but earnestly set to work to cure them.

The journey of life, and the onward march of an Order or a Nation, are not over a level plain. For a time it may be so for either, but the rugged mountain to be scaled always comes at last. The journey over the plain is not the march of heroes, nor are honor and glory won by it. Indolence may saunter over the dead level; but the climber of the mountain, whether Man, Order or Nation, must possess endurance, persistence and resolution. Oftentimes he will be forced back, but must gain strength to start anew. He must surmount obstacles of every kind and expect to encounter many dangers. Many will grow faint and weary, and halt for rest in some tempting spot that invites ease and indolent indifference. Many will essay by-ways and paths that seem easier and smoother than to go in the straight and narrow way ever upward and onward. Some of these will lose their footing and fall over the precipices that are on every side; and some the avalanches will overwhelm. To face these dangers and overcome these trials is the pride of every human life and the glory of every Order. Very little is to be learned by him who saunters over the plains and loiters in the glade or meadow.

Finally, my Brother, we are all passing away, and none of us, perhaps, will live to see the full glory of the Order. The symbolic Temple is still in building, and sometimes the hands of the workmen on the walls grow weary. The Holy Empire is not yet established. We work for the Future as the men of the Past worked for us.

Those who are Masons after us shall see, if our eyes do not behold it, the full glory of the work whose foundation has been so well laid. The leaves fall upon the root, but the tree continues to grow. The tree of Masonry continues to grow, fed by the living springs of Truth. The croak of clerical ravens and the chattering of surpliced jays may predict decay for it, but the ages will mark the periods of its growth as the years with consecutive rings do those of the oak. The lightnings of excommunication will fail to shatter its branches; no storms of persecution can uproot it and lay it prostrate. Freemasonry is of God as Truth is; the Powers of Darkness cannot prevail against it, and beneath its branches the world shall at last have peace.

Your toils as a Fellow-craft are now to begin. You have completed your work as an Apprentice

••

המדרים.
Secrecy Fidelity, Assistance, Comfort, Warning.... Obedience.

••

S∴, W∴, G∴ to ♄.

••

The Catechism is repeated before closing, when it is thought proper, and there is time; or it may be done at another meeting.

••

מדרגה שלישית.

מצפן.

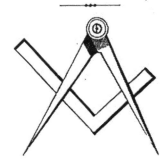

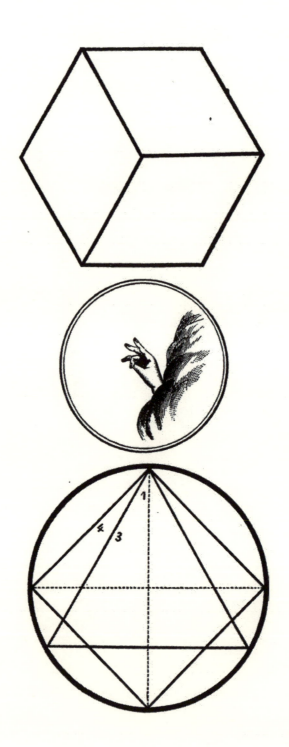

THIRD DEGREE

III.
MASTER.—MAITRE MAÇON.

ESSENTIAL INTRODUCTION.

The Preparation room is styled 'The Chamber of Reflection, It should have a sombre and gloomy appearance, being hung with dark gray cloth, and lighted by a single large Candle of yellow wax.

In the middle of this room is an Altar, eighteen inches square and three and a half feet high, covered with a black cloth. By it stands In the goblet is red wine.

There is one small table, covered with black cloth, and one chair. On the table are the working-tools of the two first Degrees, all broken. On the Altar is

In different places on the walls are the following inscriptions, painted or printed in large Letters:

'Through the frowning gates of death lies the way to eternal life,'

'Time ever digs the grave where we must lay our Sins or our Sorrows.'

'He that would die well and happily, must lead an upright life'

'Let us ever keep our house in order that we may be fit to die!'

'By a wise and virtuous life, make the best preparation for a peaceable death!'

'The Dead are with us always.'

'Blessed are the dead who die in the cause of Truth'

'All death is new Life,'

'Birth, Life Death! God the Creator, Preserver, Destroyer!' It is the Dead that govern: The Living only obey.'

'The World is filled with the Voices of the Dead.'

'The Just that is dead condemneth the Wicked that are living.'

'He that overcometh shall not be hurt of the second death.'

'To him that overcometh will I give to eat of the Tree of Life.'

'The dust returns to the earth as it was; and the Spirit unto God who gave it.'

The Senior Deacon is to prepare the Candidate. He should thoroughly understand his duty; and by appropriate remarks in regard to the solemnity and importance of the degree, should arouse expectation and excite the imagination. The grave dignity of his manner will much tend to make the ceremonial imposing.

THE MIDDLE CHAMBER.

The Lodge-room is so called. It must be wholly hung with black, both walls and ceiling, and no light be admitted from without.

Here and there, on the walls are death's heads and cross-bones, in white: and silver tears, in groups of 3, 5 and 7.

The Lodge is lighted by nine lights, three in front of each Dignitary, forming an equilateral Triangle.

On the Altar are the Hebrew Bible, the Compasses and the Square, both points of the Compasses being above the Square. On these are..........

In the middle of the Chamber is Round this

is a moveable railing, seven feet in height; and black curtains, hanging from this to the floor, surround and inclose the . . . forming a close apartment, ten or twelve feet in length and six or eight in width

TITLES.

In the Master's Lodge, the Master is styled 'Worshipful.' The Wardens are styled 'Most Venerable. The Master Masons, 'Venerable.' These titles are indispensable.

CLOTHING.

At a reception, all the Masters should be dressed in black, with a slouched black hat, and weeper of crape, white gloves, apron, and blue sash. In strictness, they ought to wear long black dominoes, and a white plume. All wear swords and sit covered. The Worshipful Master should wear a long black velvet mantle.

OPENING.

··

PRAYER.

O Lord, Thou art excellent in truth, and there is nothing great in comparison to thee! Enlighten us, we beseech Thee, in the true knowledge of Free Masonry! Let us not be numbered among those that know not Thy Statutes nor the divine Mysteries! Grant us knowledge and understanding, that we may obtain wisdom! Enable us to decipher and read the Great Book of Thy Revelation, whose pages are always open before us, and therein to find Thy Statutes and Commandments and the Keys to Thy Holy Mysteries! Bless our undertakings! Enable us to serve Thee aright! And let all our actions tend to Thy glory and to our own advancement in excellence and virtue! Help the distressed and struggling Nations to become free; and though neither our eyes nor those of our children shall behold it, make of the whole Earth thy Holy Temple: Amen!

ODE.

A MASON'S CHARITY.

'Tis not to pause, when at my door A needy brother stands;

Tis not to ask what made him poor,

Or why he help demands:

Tis not to spurn that brother's prayer,

For wrongs he may have done;

Tis not to leave him in despair,

And say that "I have none."

The voice of charity is kind,

She pleadeth nothing wrong;

To every fault she seemeth blind,

Nor vaunteth with her tongue;

In penitence she pleadeth faith,

Hope smileth at her door;

Believeth first, then gently saith,

"Go, brother! Sin no more!"

☉∴ In the Name of God and of Saint John of Scotland, and under the auspices, etc……………………….., and by virtue of the authority in me vested as Worshipful Master of this Lodge of Master-Masons, I declare……………………………………

III.
PRELIMINARIES OF RECEPTION.

A Fellow-craft cannot be raised to the third degree, until he has worked his time,—that is until he has been a Fellow-craft at least three months and a half.

This means that he has been present at seven meetings, which is indispensable (these being supposed to be held once a fort- night).

Moreover, he must be twenty-five years of age, in the absence of a dispensation as to age from an Inspector General.

When thus duly qualified, he prefers his request to ⊕.

When the matter is settled, and if the Reception is not to take place at once, the Master's Lodge will be closed, and works resumed in the Fellow-craft's degree, if these had been suspended. In that case the Fellow-crafts are called in. If the Lodge had not been working in the Fellow-craft's degree, those of Apprentice may be resumed, as they may after resuming and then closing those of Fellow-craft; and all the Brethren will re-enter.

All the Masters will be summoned to attend the Meeting when a reception is to take place. The writs of Summons will mention that a Fellow-craft is to be raised; and direct the Masters to appear in black.

At the proper hour, the Lodge may be opened in the first in- stance in the Master's degree: or it may open in the first, second and third in succession. The others are included in the Master's Lodge, and opening it, opens them.

RECEPTION.

PREPARATION OF THE CANDIDATE.

♄∴ One's own thoughts are either the best or the worst of companions…… Do not deceive yourself! Masonry is real and earnest. Its laws are stem and imperative; and the Master-Mason must not shrink from duty even if it lead him to the grave.

♄∴ It is well for man to remember that he is mortal; and to consider what is meant by his mortality. The constituents of man's body are the same as those of the bodies of the other animals. Their bones and flesh and muscles, their organs and nerves, are composed of the self-same materials as his. His blood and theirs are alike. Their hearts beat by the same mechanism, and perform the same functions as his. The anatomist discovers no radical difference between the brain of the ape and that of the man. Our food becomes part of our body, whether it be of the fruits of the earth, or the flesh of beast, bird or fish; and continually what we receive from the animals returns to them, and that which is part of our body to-day, is part of that of the bird or beast to-morrow.

Continually we eat and drink of the bodies of the dead; and the particle of matter that once was part of the body of Socrates or Plato, of Moses or of Mahomet, may to-day be part of yours or mine. The head and the body are not the Man; for these belong to the Universe of Matter, continually come and go, and after death enter into new combinations.

What then is this Self, this Me, always one and the same? Does it also end when life ceases, when the senses are annihilated, the nerves cease to convey sensations, and the body is a mass of dead matter, prepared to decay into dust or be consumed by fire?

The dog also is a Self and a Me. He thinks, remembers, dreams, reasons from cause to effect, knows the law of right and wrong, has all the senses we have, can learn and improve, is conscious of his continuing identity. Is man only a higher type of animal?

What is vitality or life? Is thought, like effervescence, perfume and taste, a result of the chemical combination of matter? If the Self or the Me is a Soul separate from the body, does it survive the body, and with what powers or faculties? Did it exist before the body? If, not content with saying what it is not, we ask our- selves what it is, what satisfactory answer does it return to us?

Is it but the vanity of man that causes him to ignore his animal nature, and to believe that he is akin to the Divinity? Is it the Self, or only the body of the Self that feels pain? Do we not feel it precisely as the animals do? They also see, hear, and think, and communicate their thoughts. If there be a Soul within us, why is it not conscious of its pre-existence? What is its origin? Was it originally part of the Deity? Is it an Emanation from Him, a spark of the Great Source of Light, or a creation from nothing, or the fruit and issue of generation? Is it, as well as the body, generated and horn?

You seek to penetrate the Inner or Greater Mysteries of Free-Masonry. Are you not already surrounded by mysteries enough; by mysteries sufficiently incomprehensible? Birth, Life, Death!—are not these mysteries appalling and tremendous enough? Perhaps you think that Masonry may explain what Faith only enables you to believe, without comprehending the enigma. Why should you imagine this: since Science and Philosophy only add to the number of those mysteries and insoluble enigmas that oppress us with a blind terror and too often sink the Soul in the profound abysses of despairing skepticism?

I promise you nothing. Does any degree of progress really bring us nearer that Light which is infinitely distant? The Secret of Masonry is perhaps only a more inexplicable mystery. Death is certain. Beyond that, all is clouds and darkness. The Stars that set in the Ocean rise again; but none of us have seen the Dead return to life. Yet the Thoughts and Influences of men survive their mortal bodies; and that is an Immortality. So the Sun's light continues, when he is beneath the earth. Life is the electric spark, the manifestation of a Spirit itself unknown.

The signs of sorrow and consternation which you witness, and the broken working-tools before you, all testify to the grief and confusion among the laborers upon the Temple. When Death, in the natural course of events, takes from us those who are dear to us, our tears flow freely, and we refuse to be comforted; but when it is inflicted by violence, the blow, more sudden and unexpected, is terrible, and wrings the Soul with agony and horror. We no longer suspect you of being an accomplice; but we must be equally assured of the innocence of your intentions and the purity of your motives

You have already heard somewhat as to the nature and purpose of those ancient Ceremonies, of which Free-Masonry is the successor. Heretofore, like the ancient Neophytes, you have been occupied with the study of moral and political truth alone. Now you are to ascend also into the region of Philosophy, the region of that higher and more sublime light, which each one values in proportion to his intellect and capacity.

••

The true object of Initiation was, to be sanctified; and to see; that is, to have just and faithful conceptions of the Deity, the knowledge of whom was the Light of the Mysteries. It was promised the Initiate at Samothrace that he should become pure and just Clemens says that by Baptism, Souls are illuminated, and led to the pure light with which mingles no darkness nor anything material. The Initiate became an Epoptes, was called a Seer. 'Hail, New- born Light!' the Initiates cried in the Mysteries of Dionusos.

Once more we remind you that the first learning in the world consisted chiefly of Symbols; and that even Modern Philosophy uses them far more than it does definitions. The wisdom of the Hindus, Chaldæans, Persians, Phoenicians, Egyptians, Hebrews, of Moses, Zarathustra, Pythagoras, Pherecydes, Socrates, Plato, of all the Ancients, that has come down to us, is symbolic. It was the mode, says Serranus, in Plato's Symposium, of the ancient Philosophers, to represent Truth by symbols and occult images.

••

To present a visible symbol to the eye of another, is not necessarily to inform him of the meaning which that symbol has to you. Hence the philosopher soon superadded to the symbols, explanations addressed to the ear, susceptible of more precision, but less effective, less obvious and impressive than the painted or sculptured forms which he endeavored to explain. Out of these explanations grew by degrees a variety of narratives, whose true object and meaning were gradually forgotten, or lost in contradictions and incongruities. And when these were abandoned, and Philosophy resorted to definitions and formulas, its language was but a more complicated symbolism, attempting in the dark to grapple with and picture ideas impossible to be ex- pressed. For as with the visible symbol, so with the word: to utter it to you does not inform you of the exact meaning which it has to me ; and thus Religion and Philosophy became , to a great extent, disputes as to the meanings of words. The most abstract expression for DEITY, which language can supply, is but a Sign or Symbol for an object beyond our comprehension, and not more truthful and adequate than the images of Osiris and Vishnu, or their names, except as being less sensuous and explicit. We avoid sensuousness, only by resorting to simple negation. We come at last to define spirit, by saying that it is not matter, Spirit is Spirit

There are dangers inseparable from symbolism, which afford an impressive lesson in regard to the similar risks attendant on the use of language. The Imagination, called in to assist the Reason, usurps its place, or leaves its ally helplessly entangled in its web. Names which stand for things are confounded with them; the means are mistaken for the end; the instrument of interpretation for the object; and thus symbols come to usurp an independent character as Truths and Persons. Though perhaps a necessary path, they were a dangerous one by which to approach the Deity; in which many, says Plutarch, ' mistaking the sign for the thing signified, fell into a ridiculous superstition; while others, in avoiding one extreme, plunged into the no less hideous gulf of irreligion and impiety.'

It is through the Mysteries, Cicero says, that we have learned the first principles of life; wherefore the term 'Initiation' is used with good reason; and they not only teach us to live more happily and agreeably, but they soften the pains of death by the hope of a better life hereafter.

The Mysteries were a sacred Drama, exhibiting some legend significant of Nature's change, of the visible Universe in which the Divinity is revealed, and whose import was in many respects as open to the Pagan as to the Christian. Nature is the great Teacher of Man; for it is the Revelation of God. It neither dogmatizes nor attempts to tyrannize by compelling to a particular creed or special interpretation. It presents its symbols to us, and adds nothing by way of explanation. It is the text without the commentary: and, as we well know, it is chiefly the commentary and gloss that lead to error and heresy and persecution. The earliest instructors of mankind not only adopted the lessons of Nature, but as far as possible adhered to her method of im- parting them. In the Mysteries, beyond the ancient tradition or sacred and enigmatic recitals of the Temples, few explanations were given to the spectators, who were left, as in the School of Nature, to make inferences for themselves. No other method could have suited every degree of cultivation and capacity. To employ Nature's universal symbol- ism instead of the technicalities of language, rewards the humblest inquirer, and discloses its secrets to everyone in proportion to his preparatory training and his power to comprehend them. If their philosophical meaning was above the comprehension of some, their moral and political meanings were within the reach of all.

These mystic shows and performances were not the reading of a lecture, but the opening of a problem. Requiring research, they were calculated to arouse the dormant intellect. They implied no hostility to Philosophy, because Philosophy is the great Expounder of Symbolism; although its ancient interpretations were often ill-founded and in- correct. The alteration from symbol to dogma is fatal to beauty of expression, and leads to intolerance and assumed infallibility.

Masonry still follows the ancient method of teaching. Her symbols are her instruction. The Lectures are but hints and helps towards the interpretation of her symbols. Each Initiate must study, interpret and develop the symbols for himself.

■ ▪ ■

The Mysteries were carried into every country, in order that, without disturbing the absurd popular beliefs, Truth, the Arts and the Sciences might be known to those who were capable of understanding them, and to maintain the true or sacred Doctrine incorrupt, which the people, prone to superstition and idolatry, have in no age been able to do; nor, as many strange aberrations and superstitions of the present day prove, any more now than heretofore

For in all ages the profoundest truths have been wisely covered from the Common People, as with a vail. By these, everywhere, what was originally revered as the symbol of a higher Principle, became gradually confounded or identified with the object itself, and was worshiped; until this prone- ness to error led to the most degraded form of idolatry. And where, at the present day, they no longer worship idols and images made with the hands, they form and fashion ideas, images and idols in their minds, which are not the Deity or like the Deity; and worship them. The common notions of our own day are as absurd as those of Paganism: and in the vulgar mind the same efficacy is attributed to rites and ceremonies as at any time in the ancient World. Still it continues literally true that most men worship Baal and not God.

■ ▪ ■

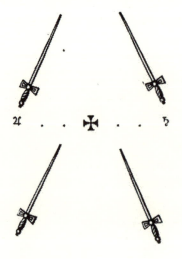

ג . . ב . . א

Remember now thy Creator in the days of thy youth while the evil days come not, nor the years draw nigh when thou shalt say, I have no pleasure in them ; while the Sun, or the Light, or the Moon, or the Stars be not darkened, nor the clouds return after the rain; in the day when the keepers of the House shall tremble, and the strong men shall bow themselves, and the grinders cease because they are few, and those that look out of the windows be darkened ; and the doors shall be shut in the streets when the sound of the grinding is low; and he shall rise up at the voice of the bird, and all the daughters of music shall be brought low. Also when they shall be afraid of that which is high, and fears shall be in the way, and the almond-tree shall flourish, and the grasshopper shall be a burden, and desire shall fail; because Man goeth to his long home, and the Mourners go about the streets: or ever the silver cord be loosed, or the golden bowl be broken at the fountain, or the wheel broken at the cistern. Then shall the dust re- turn to the earth as it was; and the Spirit shall return unto God who gave it.

MUSIC.

....

Three Planets were deemed by the Ancients to be above and three below the Sun: and the natural order of all, proceeding upward from the Earth, was deemed to be, the Moon, Mercury, Venus, the Sun, Mars, Jupiter, Saturn. To these, in the same order, were assigned the Seven Archangels, Tsaphiel, Raphael, Hamaliel, Zarakhiel, Auriel, Gabriel and Michael. All these are combinations of other words with AL or EL, the name of the Deity originally worshiped by the Hebrews.

God, in the Hebrew writings, is continually symbolized by Light. The Sun was regarded as His visible Image. The 'Word of God' is explained by Philo in Eusebius, to be the Universal and Invisible Light, Source, Sub- stance or Essence of the Light cognizable by the Senses, and which shines forth from the Planets and Stars. The word 'Light' was used, for want of any other or better, to express the Essence, of which visible Light is the manifestation. The Deity was better expressed, as the occult essential Fire, of which Flame is the action, Light the outflowing or manifestation.

The worship of Fire and Light was the basis of all the religions of Antiquity. Agni, the Fire, and Indra, the Light, were the highest Deities of our ancestors the Aryans. And when Zarathustra, among the Bactro- or Irano — Aryans, imagined a spiritual God, Ahura Mazda, superior to these, and Author and Creator of the Universe, with his Seven Emanations , the Amesha-

Cpentas, the second of these was Asha-Vahista, the Spirit of Fire; and Fire is continually called in the Zend-Avesta, the Son of Ahura-Mazda. The Persian Mithra was the Sun, but the original Bactrian and Iranian Mithra was the Morning-Star.

In the Vedic or Vaidik Hymns, composed at least 4,000 and probably 5,000 years before our Era, the Sun, Moon, Planets and Stars are bodies by which Agni and Indra, Fire and Light, manifest themselves. They are, all, Agni and Indra, in fact, limited and defined by form and body.

The Avesta calls the Sun the body of Ahura-Mazda. The Indo-Aryans had the same idea. By the Helleno-Aryans the Sun was regarded as the visible image of the Deity.

The Seven Amesha-Cpentas, or Divine Emanations, known to the Hebrews by their Median captivity, became the seven Archangels, of which one was assigned to each of the seven bodies, formerly called 'The Planets;'—The Sun, the Moon, Mercury, Venus, Mars, Jupiter and Saturn. They were still emanations or rays from the Invisible Essential Light, which was the Very Deity,—rays by which the Deity was manifested and shone forth, each being the Deity manifested in one mode and characteristic.

Accordingly, each Archangelic Name has a reference to this Light, which is the Deity. Tsaphiel means The Splendor of Al: Raphael, The Healing of Al, reminding us of 'The Sun of Righteousness rising with healing in his wings:' Hamaliel, the Benignity of Al: Zarakhiel, the Rising of Al: Auriel, the Light of AL: Gabriel, the Potency of Al: and Michael, the Semblance or Image of Al.

On all the Monuments of Mithra, we see by the side of that God seven altars or pyres, consecrated to the seven Planets ; and these and the seven Candlesticks represented the seven Spheres or Vessels that shed abroad in the Universe the ethereal Light. By these altars the seven Angels are seen. Sometimes, instead of the altars are seen seven Stars, symbolized by the seven gates of the Mithriac cave, through which the Initiates passed; and which passages are represented by your journeys.

The Ancients thought that the natural home of the Soul of Man was in the highest regions of the Universe, in the Sphere of the fixed Stars. Hence it was held to have descended through the seven Planetary Spheres, to illumine the body, to communicate to it form and movement, to vivify and animate it; in the same manner as, when the Universe of Matter was a shapeless Chaos, THE BREATH OF GOD *moved* on the surface of the abyss.

The Soul tends to re-ascend, as soon as it can free itself from the impediment of Matter. The re-ascension of each Soul would be more or less tedious and laborious, according as it was more or less clogged by the gross impediments of its sins and vices.

Except for the gravest sins there could be expiation; and by penance, repentance, acts of beneficence and prayer, symbolized by the tests of *water*, *air* and *fire*, the Soul could be purified, and rise toward the ethereal regions : but grave crimes were *mortal* sins, beyond the reach of such remedies.

∎∎∎

The visible World is the image of the invisible World. The essence of the human Soul is the image of God; and its home is above the Stars.

The Equinoxes were the gates through which Souls passed to and fro, between the Hemisphere of Light, and that of Darkness. Near each of these gates passed the Galaxy; and it was termed "The Pathway of Souls."

The symbolic image of this passage among the Stars, was a ladder reaching from earth to Heaven, divided into seven Steps or Stages, to each of which was a gate, and at the summit an eighth, that of the fixed Stars. You have already seen this mystic ladder. It is by knowledge as well as morals the Soul ascends toward the Stars, and climbs the skies to its home. An emanation of the ethereal Fire, exiled from the luminous starry region, it descended through the planetary gates, and by the equinoctial and solstitial doors, along the Milky Way, to be immured in the prison-house of Matter. There the body is its prison, until it shall at last return to its place of origin, its home, through the Constellations and planetary Spheres.

Through the Gate of Capricorn, along the Galaxy, and by the way of the Seven Spheres it must ascend. To re ascend to the Unity of its Source, it must pass through a series of trials and migrations. The scene of these is the grand Sanctuary of Initiations, the World. Their primary agents are the Elements: the means, are the sorrows, the trials and the calamities of Life.

Thus the theories of the Ancients were not mere barren speculation: but a study of the means for arriving at the great object proposed, the perfecting of the Soul, and, as a consequence, that of morals and society and the State. The Earth, to them, was not the Soul's Home, but its place of exile. Its home and birth-place was Heaven. To purify this Soul of its passions, and weaken the empire of the body over it, to give him true happiness here below, and expedite his re-ascension to his home, was the object of initiation.

∎∎∎

Tour Soul has passed, symbolically, in its ascent toward its home, through the Spheres of Saturn, Venus, and Jupiter, called by the Hebrews, Sabatai, Nogah and Tsaduc, symbolized by the metals lead, copper and tin; and their colors black, blue and scarlet

At the Sphere of Saturn, the Ancients said, the Soul, ascending, parted with its Falsehood and Deceit. Are you now free from these most common vices of humanity, which infect alike the conduct of the individual and the policy of the State?

Look around you, and see how few men are habitually and perfectly frank, sincere, true and loyal! Interrogate yourself, and admit that you have too often, under temptation, and to attain a coveted object, been false and deceitful.

What is more common among men than the pretense of friendship, coupled with the reality of enmity or ill-will! What more common than professions belied by practice! How constantly are the Masonic pretenses and professions of brotherhood mere idle, empty words!

Remember that the Mason is, above all things, a true man and a loyal Citizen. Falsehood and deceit, in man or Nation, are ignoble and dishonorable. Let them become common as they will, until a profitable lie has its market-price, and falsehoods swarm in the putrid carcass of the body-politic; until fraudulent bankruptcies no longer diminish respectability, and no trust is too sacred to be violated, no oath too solemn to be broken, no pledge of public or private honor strong enough to bind the Soul; until the State or Nation contemptuously disregards her pledges, violates the obligation of her contracts, does more than that for which she incarcerates her citizens as swindlers ; still, if you believe you have a living Soul, and if you hope for its re- ascension to its home beyond the Stars, you must purify it of Falsehood, Fraud and Deceit.

••

At the Sphere of Venus, said the Ancients, the Soul, ascending toward its home, shakes off its sensual Appetites and Passions

••

The appetites and passions are the gift of God, for good and wise purposes. Allowed to predominate and control, they become our Tyrants, and are frightful vices and leprous diseases of the Soul. Lust and gluttony and drunkenness brutalize the Soul equally with the body, and make greatness and goodness impossible. They turn Wisdom into Folly, and Intellect into Idiocy. They debauch, corrupt and infect the whole Man. But when the just equilibrium is preserved between the appetites and passions, the Moral Sense and the Reason, the first are spurs and incentives to exertion, the springs of vigorous Manliness, the sources of love, effort and heroism.

Vice and Luxury have in all ages sapped the foundations of States. Manliness and virtue, the family affections, Temperance, Frugality and Economy are the only sure preservatives of Republics. Debauchery and vice are a syphilitic poison in the arteries of a Commonwealth. Extravagance and luxury lead to dishonesty and peculation and to the prostitution of place and office; to lavish expenditures, oppressive debts, ruinous taxation, and the ultimate subjugation of Labor by Capital. Public corruption is the twin of private dishonesty.

If you would truly become a Master Mason, purify your own Soul, and resolve to do your utmost to purify the State, of profligacy and debauchery. Keep your appetites and passions ever under due control. Be not their slave, but their Master. Discourage vice, luxury and extravagance among the people and in the State, and remember that a Nation also has a Soul that may be brutalized; and that if the baser animals have their types among men, so also they have among States. Remember that public debt and the luxury of the rich breed pauperism among the People, and diseases that at last culminate in revolution; and that in- variably, the anarchy of the revolution of the poor against the rich, leads to the tyranny of the Despot and the atrocities of absolute Power.

At the Sphere of Jupiter, the ascending Soul parted, it was said, with its Avarice. It is a vice which Civilization, Commerce and Freedom largely develop. Wealth always tends, in prosperous States, to become the supreme Good, the highest merit, the aggregate, of all the virtues; and Poverty to be less a misfortune than a misdemeanor. Inordinately valued, and giving power and consequence, Money becomes a God.

Free of avarice himself, the Mason should endeavor to shame into deeds of beneficence those who are not so. It matters little to the poor who are succored, whether it is mere ostentation or genuine charity that relieves them. He should spread the example of his benevolence beyond the circle of those only who are wise and good, and every day widen the sphere of his usefulness among his fellow-creatures, convinced that the life he will them lead will be the most acceptable of all lives to the Supreme Being.

The Hebrew name of Jupiter is Tsaduc, the Just. Let the Mason whose Soul has passed symbolically through that planetary Sphere, strive, by honest exertion and honorable means, to secure a competency for himself and for his children, since that is laudable and just and wise: but let him not become diseased with the leprosy of avarice, nor seek to amass wealth by those speculations which enrich one by the robbery of many, or by the loss and calamity of the State. Let him aid his Country to attain greatness and secure prosperity by the ways of justice and honor and noble and heroic enterprise, and not by the acquisition of territory wrested or stolen from the weak, or by a commercial supremacy obtained by a selfish policy, and retained by disregarding all the divine obligations of sympathy, justice and generosity.

....

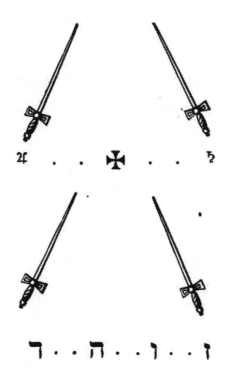

MUSIC.

....

According to Plato, the Soul cannot re-enter into Heaven, until the revolutions of the Universe shall have restored it to its primitive condition, and purified it from the effects of its connection with the four elements.

....

If you would understand the ancient Mind, and be enabled to interpret the allegories and explore the symbols in which the old Sages endeavored to delineate the ideas that struggled within them for utterance, and could be only in- adequately expressed by language, you must study the connection between the secret science and mysterious emblems of Initiation, and the Heavens, the Spheres, and the Constellations.

....

At the Sphere of Mercury, the Soul was said to part with all inclination to Injustice and Hypocrisy.

Nothing is so difficult as for a man to be entirely just If he be so in his conduct, no man is always so in his opinions, and his judgment of the conduct of others. To nothing are we so prone, as to uncharitable judgment; and yet there is nothing of which we so much complain, and with so much reason, against men and public opinion, in our own case. We know that even when there is the most apparent reason for harsh judgment against us, there are extenuating circumstances unknown to the world, good motives at bot- tom, stress of temptation, weakness and error more than intentional wrong, which if the world knew, it ought in jus- tice to modify if not to reverse its stem and pitiless judgment. How rarely do we presume that others whom we condemn have like excuses or justification! The only just judgment is that which is charitable and merciful Even the Infinite and Perfect Justice is in equilibrium with the Infinite and Perfect Mercy; the Infinite Wisdom above both, holding the beam of the balance.

....

We need no other definition of Justice than that of the great Teacher who gave his Name to a Religion that now for the most part repudiates his precepts : "All things what- soever ye would that men should do to you, do ye even so to them ; for this is the Law aud the Prophets"

....

Avoid, therefore, for the future, as one purified and sanctified, all injustice, extortion and hypocrisy: and as a Citizen of the State help to cast out of office and power all who advocate and countenance injustice, all who flatter the people and mislead them to betray them; all who clothe schemes of unjust National aggrandizement in the livery of the apostolate of Freedom, and to the shame of National robbery, add the utter baseness of a sanctified hypocrisy.

At the Sphere of Mars, the Soul, ascending, was said to part with the vices of Revenge, Anger, Ingratitude, Impatience and Querulousness, resuming in their stead its original virtues of Mercy, Forgiveness, Forbearance, Gratitude, Patience and Equanimity.

"Love your enemies," said The Great Teacher; "bless them that curse you! Do good to them that hate you! Pray for them which despitefully use you and persecute you! " Do this, He said, "that ye may be the children of your Father which is in Heaven; for He maketh His Sun to rise on the Evil and on the Good, and Sendeth rain on the Just and on the Unjust"

■■■

If it be not in human Nature not to take revenge by way of punishment, let the Mason truly consider that in doing so he is God's agent, and so let his revenge be measured by Justice and tempered by Mercy. The law of God is that the consequences of wrong and cruelty and crime shall be their punishment; and the injured and the wronged and the indignant are as much His instruments to enforce that law, as the diseases and public detestation, and the verdict of History and the execration of Posterity are. No one will say that the Inquisitor who has racked and burned the innocent ; the Spaniard who has hewed Indian infants, living, into pieces with his sword, and fed the mangled limbs to his blood-hounds; the military Tyrant who has shot men without trial, the knave who has robbed or betrayed his State, the fraudulent banker or bankrupt who has beggared orphans, the public officer who has violated his oath, the Judge who has sold injustice, the Legislator who has enabled incapacity to work the ruin of the State, ought not to be punished. Let them be so; and let the injured or the sympathizing be the instruments of God's just vengeance; but always out of a higher feeling than mere personal revenge.

A querulous impatience argues an entire absence of heroism. To complain of and repine at the dispensations of Providence, is worse than a folly. Patience and Equanimity are the inseparable attributes of a truly great soul 'The Commandment is a lamp,' says the Wise King; 'and the Law is Light: and reproofs of instruction the way of life.' All must bear the cross; the wisest bear it most patiently. After all, the sadness's of life help to sweeten the bitter cup of death. 'Happy is the man,' said Eliphas, the friend of Job, 'whom God correcteth; therefore despise not thou the chastening of the Almighty' Omnipotent Wisdom created the Human Race. To exist at all, a being of spirit and body united, Man could not but be made subject to pain and sickness, to evils and deprivations and calamities. After all, is it not always better to have suffered than not to have lived at all? Suffer as we may, lose as we may, we still cling to life, finding in it something to outweigh our sufferings and sorrows.

———

At the Sphere of the Moon, called in the Hebrew Labanah, Whiteness, the Soul, ascending, was said to lay aside its Prejudices and Preconceptions. These are inseparable from us in this life. No man is without them: there are too few who not slaves to them. In all ages they have led to bigotry and persecution; and men are generally most bigoted, in proportion to the want of real foundation for their faith. One is not satisfied to believe that he is in possession of the Truth, unless he can also persuade or compel others to follow and adopt his faith.

••
―――――――

At the Sphere of the Sun, called in the Hebrew Shemesh, the Soul, ascending, was said to part with its aspirations for Greatness and Empire. Man naturally covets influence, power, control and dominion over man, and is not content with controlling the body, unless he can also control the Soul. Hence the love of unlawful and unreasonable power, and Tyranny and Usurpation. Nations covet empire and dominion. Propagandists equally of Freedom and Despotism, they are not only bigoted and persecuting like individuals, but their lust for power and pre-eminence is insatiate.

••

Let every Mason be content to be Monarch over himself ! Let him seek to control no man against his will, to coerce no man to believe as he believes. Even in a republic, let him tolerate monarchical opinions. Let him, to convert men from error, use only the weapons of argument and reason! Let him, as a Citizen, hold that greatness and empire are not essential to the prosperity of States; that small States, free, are better and happier than large ones enslaved; and that consolidation by conquest, is like uniformity of faith produced by persecution. The man and the Nation that would rise into the highest sphere of excellence, must be free from ambition and the insane desire to rule; since from these flow all manner of injustices, oppressions and tyrannies, ending at last in calamities unutterable ; in Rome, under Vitellius and Domitian, Spain under the Bourbons, the Ottoman Empire existing by sufferance, a Church with the will but without the power to persecute, the Throne over the Volcano, and a Republic cemented by blood, and weak in all its apparent grandeur, by the terrible hostility of hate.

At the Sphere of the Sun, you are in the region of Light.

••

The God of the Hebrews was not only Yehuah, but the Lord of the Celestial Armies, the Alohim, Adonai, Al Shadai, Aloh, Aliun, AL, the Malak, Yehuah-Elohim, Adon-Tsabaoth. 'Out of Ziun, the

Perfection of Beauty, He shone.' 'He sits in the Heavens: He is in His holy Temple; His Throne is in the Heavens: He lights the lamp of the Faithful, and enlightens their darkness.' 'He is,' says David, 'my Light and my Salvation.' He is a Sun and a shield. He is to be an everlasting Light and a Glory; a Light to those sitting in darkness: He sends out His Light and His Truth to lead His servants. 'Thou that dwellest between the Cherubim,' they cried to Him, 'shine forth! Cause Thy face to shine! And we shall be saved!' He covers Himself with light as with a garment, and makes his Angels Spirits, and his Ministers a flaming fire. God is the Lord which hath showed us light. His word is a lamp to the feet and a light to the path of the Faithful'

• •

הנררם.

Secrecy. .. .Obedience   Duties toward a Brother—to his Family.

• •

You are still in search of Light. "The King of Kings and Lord of Lords," Paul says to Timotheus, "Who alone has eternal existence, dwelleth in the Light into which no mortal can come." "In the World," says Saint John, "was life, and that life was the Light of men, the true Light, which lighteth every man that cometh into the World." "He that doeth what is Bight and True, cometh to the Light, that his actions may be manifestly seen to accord with His divine will."

• •

Duty and danger go always, in this world, hand in hand; and the Master Mason, Apostle of Light and Liberty, must ever say, and on this saying ever act; 'The mean consideration of my own safety shall never be put in the balance against my duty. I will own no superior but the laws: nor bend the knee to anyone but Him who made me.' Death is not, by far, the greatest evil that can befall a man. To betray a trust or violate an obligation is a greater misfortune than to die. In defense of his own rights of free action, speech and conscience, or of the civil and religious rights of his people, with the God of Armies on his side, the Mason will not fear the hour of trial, 'for though the hosts of his enemies should cover the field like locusts, yet the Sword of the Lord and of Gideon shall prevail'

PRAYER.

Our Father, who art in Heaven, hear our reverent supplication! Thou who dwellest in the Light, illumine the soul and strengthen the heart of this Candidate! Help him to keep his solemn obligations! Remind him continually of them, that he may not forget them or become indifferent or lukewarm and so incur the guilt of perjury! Enable him ever to prefer danger to dishonor, and martyrdom to betrayal of his trust or abandonment of the just cause of the People! Guide and protect us and all good Masons in the discharge of our solemn and sacred duties! Give us courage to prefer a glorious death to a base life! Make prosperous and effectual the good work of Masonry, and let it be Thy instrument to aid in the regeneration of Humanity! Make it a force and power! Direct its labors and shape its courses for good! Enlighten us! Illumine us! Instruct us! And let us be able to thank Thee, when we come to die, that by Thy Grace and Favor we have not lived in vain! Amen!

All: So mote it be! Amen!

The past Centuries return: the Works of the First Temple rise around us in all their grandeur: The Divine Presence dwells again between the extended wings of the Cherubim in the Holy of Holies, on the Mercy-Seat: the Past has become the Present; and the Present the Future.

MUSIC.
X∴ LEGEND AND DRAMA.

When David the King of Israel had brought the Ark of God from the house of Abinadab in Gibeah to the house of Obed-Edom, and thence into the City of David, he proposed to build a house in which it might dwell; but Yehuah, by Nathan his prophet, forbade it, saying to him, that when his days should be fulfilled, and he should sleep with his fathers, his Son should build a House for Yehuah.

Afterward David purchased the threshing-floor of Oman or Araunah, the Jebusite, on Mount Moriah, to set up there an altar unto Yehuah ; the Tabernacle, the Ark and the Altar of Sacrifices being then upon the hill at Gabaon. Then he prepared materials for the building of the Temple, with the help of the workmen sent him by Khairfum, King of Tsur, hewn stones, iron and brass, and timbers of cedars in abundance, with a hundred thousand talents of gold and a million talents of silver; saying to Solomon that Yehuah had forbidden him to build the House, because he had shed much blood and made great wars ; and giving it to him in charge that he should build the House of Yehuah his Alohim; and to the Princes of Israel that they should help Solomon to build the House, the Sanctuary of Yehuah-Alohim, and bring the Ark of the Covenant of Yehuah, and the holy vessels of the Alohim, into the House to be so built to the name of Yehuah.

Accordingly, in the four hundred and eightieth year after the Exodus from Egypt, in the fourth year of the reign of Solomon, in the month Zif, which is the second month, he began to build the House of Yehuah. Already he had sent to Khairum King of Tsur, the firm friend and ally of his father, requesting to be furnished with Tsidunians hewers, to hew cedar-trees for the House, upon Mount Lebanon.

----------Khairum cheerfully granted what was asked, and directed that his servants should bring the cedar and pine timbers from Lebanon to the Sea, and convey them on rafts along the coast to Yapu, whence they could be taken to Jerusalem; Solomon paying for this service with wheat and oil.

Also King Khairum or Khurum sent to King Solomon a skillful workman, a man of judgment, also named Khairum or Khurum, the son of a woman of the Tribe of Dan or Naphtali, whose father was a Tsurian; a skillful workman in metals, stone and wood, and in embroidery and carving, who cast the great columns for the main entrance, and made the furniture and vessels.

To procure the materials, Solomon drafted 30,000 men of the different Tribes, and divided them into three classes, each of 10,000. Each class labored on Lebanon one month and was at home two months, in every three. There were also 70,000 bearers of burdens, and 80,000 hewers in the mountains; for Solomon built not only the Temple, but also a Palace for himself, and the

House of the Forest of Lebanon, larger than the Temple. 3,300 Officers superintended the workmen: and so the great costly hewn stones and the timbers were prepared.

---------- Thus there were, bearers of burdens, Sabal,   70,000

---------- Hewers in the Mountains, Khatsabim   80,000

---------- Superintendents or Overseers, Manatzkhim,   3,300

---------- Besides the 10,000 Israelites and the Men of Gebal sent by the King of Tsur.

The three classes were not only distinguished from each other by the Nature of their employment, but the Sabal and Khatsabim were foreigners. They were the Apprentices; the Men of Israel and Gebal the Fellow-crafts; and the Manatzkhim the Masters of the work.

Those of each degree, it is said, had signs and words by which to recognize each other, and to enable them to receive their wages.

To receive these, the Apprentices, it is said, congregated at the Column Jachin; the Fellow-crafts at the Column Boaz; the Masters in the middle Chamber.

The foundation was laid, as we have said, in the second month of the fourth year of Solomon's reign. The Temple was completely finished in the eighth month, Bul or Khesvan, of the eleventh year of his reign; seven years and six months having thus been occupied in its erection. On the second day of the second month, Zif or Ijar, of the year 1012 before Christ, the first stone of the foundation was laid. In the seventh month, Ethanim or Tisri, of the year 1004 before Christ, the House of God was solemnly dedicated, and the Ark of the Covenant placed in the Holy of Holies.

But in the meantime, as our Masonic tradition informs us, a tragical scene had been enacted in the unfinished Temple.

It was promised by King Solomon, that when the Temple should be finished and dedicated, the most skillful and faithful Fellow-crafts should be raised to the rank of Master Mason, and invested with the Master's Word, with which, though aliens and not Hebrews, they might travel into foreign countries and earn Master's Wages.

Fifteen of these Fellow-crafts, when the Temple was nearly finished, desiring to return to their own country, because they were weary of the work and had not been industrious enough, nor were skillful enough, to expect to be selected to receive the Master's degree, plotted together to force Khurum, the Master of the Workmen, to make known to them the Word; intending, when they had forced it from him, to return secretly to their native countries.

Twelve of these, repenting, failed to meet the others in the Temple, at the time agreed upon for putting their plot into execution. The others, though disappointed, persisted.

They were brothers, whose names are said to have been Yubela, Yubelo, and Yubelum. These are symbolic, as you will learn hereafter. In other forms of the legend, Yubela is called Romvel or Guibs; Yubelo, Hobhen or Gravelot; and Yubelum, Abiram, Abibal, and Akirop. To one or the other, also, we find the names of Oterfurth, Oterfut [or Otterfoot] and Schterke, assigned.

Yubela……………………………………………… at the South Gate.

Yubelo……………………………………………… at the West Gate.

Yubelum……………………………………………at the East Gate.

....

♩♩♩♩♩♩♩♩♩♩♩

....

EVENING HYMN OF THE WORKMEN.

Abide with me! —fast falls the Even-tide;
The darkness thickens: **LORD!** With me abide! — When other helpers fail, and comforts flee,
Help of the helpless, O abide with me!

———

Swift to its close ebbs out life's little day: Earth's joys grow dim, its glories pass away; Change and decay in all around I see:

O Thou who changest not, abide with me!

───────────

I fear no foe, with Thee at hand to bless;—

Ills have no weight, and tears no bitterness.

Where is Death's sting; where, Grave, thy victory? I triumph still, if God abides with me.

───────────

Reveal Thyself before my closing eyes!

Shine through the gloom, and point me to the skies! Heaven's morning breaks, and Earth's vain shadows flee;

In life, in death, O Lord, abide with me!

───────────

• •

It is a dark and cloudy night

The better for our purpose.

• •

• •

○   ○   ○

• •

• •

It is the third hour, and yet the Most Worshipful Master Khurum hath not come to the Temple, and the workmen know not how to proceed with their work.

••

The most careful search has been made by all the work-men, within and around the Temple, and throughout the City; but the Master cannot be found.

••

♪♪♪

☽∴ O our Lord the King, let not thy anger consume thy Servants, though we have sinned against thee and in the sight of God. We have repented, and our hearts are dead within us. We who are twelve, with three other of our fellows, wearying of the work, and fearing we should not be found worthy to receive the Master's degree at the dedication of the Temple, conspired together to compel the Most Worshipful Master Khurum, by threats of violence, to make known to us the Master's Word, in-tending then to flee to foreign countries, and there be enabled, as Sons of the Light, to earn Master's Wages. We twelve, reflecting upon the enormity of the attempt, repented and abandoned our wicked purpose. But since our Most Worshipful Master is not to be found, we fear that the other three have carried their purpose into effect, and to conceal their crime have taken the Master's life.

••

☿∴ Inquiry has been made among the workmen; and the three Edomitish brothers are not to be found, nor have they to-day been seen of any one.

••

To obtain forgiveness for evil deeds or counsels, it is not enough to have repented. Reparation and good deeds are also needed. Are you willing to search, even as far as the Sea-coast and the Desert, for the Master or his body, and for those whose accomplices you were to have been, and to make them captives, even at the peril of death?

••

☉∴ My Brother Azariah, divide these twelve Fellow-crafts into four parties of three each. Let three go to the North, as far as Galilee; three to the South, beyond Hebron and Carmel; three to the East, as far as the river Jordan and along the shores of the Sea of Sadam; and three to the West, as far as the Sea-coast and to Yapu. If they find the Master's body, let them carefully examine it, and bring to us whatsoever they may find upon it, bestowing it in safety and honor where we may go and give it burial. If they overtake the fugitives, let them take them captive, or die in the attempt. If they do their duty manfully and faithfully, they will have atoned for their fault and shall be forgiven, and may hope to attain to the

■ ■

♪♪

♂ ∴ Our Lord the King, we are the three Fellow-crafts who were sent to the west in search of the body of our Master and of the Edomitish fugitives. When we had journeyed a day, and were near the Sea-coast, we heard the first tidings. Meeting a wayfaring man, we learned that he had, some hours before, met three men, foreigners who swore by Baal, and seemed to be laborers, on the way to Yapu; who, learning from him that no vessels were about to sail from that port, seemed troubled and alarmed, and with many imprecations turned back toward the hill country of Samaria. Believing these to be the fugitives, we hastened after them that night and the next day, and stopping at nightfall to rest in the mountains, we heard voices of men conversing, as we discovered, in a cave nearby. We listened and heard one say, "What folly to think that such a man as the Master Khurum would betray his trust through fear of death!"

----------Then another said; "We have stained our hands with his blood for nought."

----------And the third; "Now we shall never obtain the

Master's Word: and no doubt the Avenger of blood is already on our track."

----------Then the first voice said; "O wretched Jubela, thou art lost. For murder and sacrilege, the punishment is death by fire in the Valley of Hinnom: to be hunted like a wolf, and then slowly, dying a thousand deaths, to be burned to ashes……."

■ ■

Alas! O Lord my God! Was there no help for the Widow's Son? The Master Khurum is no more! But he died bravely, refusing to betray his trust, and shall ever be to Masons an emblem of

Fidelity and Honor. The Murderers cannot escape. The unseen Avenger of blood pursues them. I have forbidden the sailing of vessels from any of my ports, and sent messengers with the tidings to my Brother Khurum of Tsur, and all the tributary Kings and Princes, and even to Damascus and to the King of Egypt. When they are apprehended, each shall receive the punishment he invoked upon himself. The steps of Justice are soft, but sure. Meanwhile, as soon as the other nine Fellow- crafts return, and if they have not found the body of our Worshipful Master, let the twelve again go forth, divided into four parties as before, and search in every direction, for the distance of a day's journey from the City, while all the Masters pray to the God of Israel to make known to us where we may find the body.

・・・

MUSIC.

☉∴ Venerable Masters, my Brethren, I have called you together from the River to the land of the Philistines, and unto the border of Egypt, in consequence of the murder of our Most Worshipful Master Khurum, and to assist me in finding his body and giving it Masonic burial. Let the Lodge of Sorrow and Mourning be duly tiled.

・・・

◯∴ As the Sun is in the South at high Noon, so I stand there to oversee the workmen, and call them from labor to refreshment, and from refreshment to labor again, that the Holy Temple may in due time be finished.

・・・

⊕∴ as the Sun stands in the gate of the West to close the day, so I stand there to close the daily labor of the workmen, and on the sixth day of each week to pay them their wages, that on the Holy Sabbath they may be content.

・・・

⊕∴ As the Sun stands in the gates of the Morning to open the day and dispel the darkness, so stands the Most Worshipful Master in the East, to open and instruct his Lodge, and cause the Good to triumph over the Evil.

☉∴ The Most Worshipful Master stands in the East and the Wardens stand in their stations. Let the Most Venerable Brethren Tsaduc and Abiathar, the Priests, offer up their prayers. Kneel, my Brethren.

[All kneel, and ♄ and ☌ offer up this prayer:

PRAYER.

♄∴ O Sovereign and Supreme God of Israel, hear the prayer of thy servants in their distress!

----------- ☌∴ O Thou whom no man hath seen or can see, help us in our Affliction: Calamity has fallen upon us, and the Waters of Sorrow flow over our heads.

----------- ♄∴ Thou art our life and our salvation! Have mercy upon us, O Lord, and help us in our distress!

----------- ☌∴. Let thy Loving-kindness encompass us about, and Thy tender Mercies give us strength! We acknowledge our transgressions: our sins are ever before us.

-----------♄∴ Wash us from our iniquities, and cleanse us from our sins!

----------- ☌∴ Create in us clean hearts! And renew a right spirit within us!

-----------♄∴ Cast us not away from thy presence! And take not Thy Holy Spirit from us!

----------- ☌∴ Open our lips, and our mouths shall show forth Thy praise.

-----------♄∴ Amen!

----------- ☌∴ So MOTE it be!

. . . .

☉∴ ………select nine of the Masters, and let three search within the City, three on the North and East of it, and three on the West and South. If they find the body, let them carefully examine it, and if there be upon it any……………..   let them bring it up to us, and carefully note the place where the body lies, that they may conduct us to it.

MUSIC.

••

☉∴ Most Worshipful Master, we being ordered to go without the City and search on the West and South of it, went forth at the gate of Yapu, and thence by the foot of Mount Ziun into the Valley of Hinnom, and finding nothing, returned, to enter in at the gate of Ziun: but when we had ascended the Mount of Ziun, and were near to the Tomb of thy father, David the King, we came to a place upon the brow of the Mount, where the earth seemed to have been newly stirred, and upon examining found it to be a grave. Not doubting that the murderers had buried the Master there, and the distance from the Temple not being great, we thought it our duty, before disturbing the grave, to return and make known our discovery, that you might do what should seem good in your sight. And that we might readily find the grave, we took and placed, upon a mound at the head of it, a small bush of acacia.

••

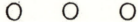

FUNERAL CHANT AND HYMN.

Mane nobiscum, Domine, quoniam advesperascit, et inclinata est jam dies laboriosœ hujus vitœ.

1.

The Cross, if rightly borne, shall be No burden, but support to thee.

O brave and true man, upon whom Is laid the Cross of cruel doom.

Nunquid narrabit aliquis in sepulcro misericordiam Tuam, et veritatem in pulvere?

2.

Rather to die than trust betray,

Than promise break or falsehood say,

So the heroic Master chose,

And bade defiance to his foes.

Ut omnibus benefactoribus nostris œterna bona retribuas, pro beneficiis, quœ nobis largiti sunt in terris, prœmia œterna consequantur in codis.

3.

His was the seed-time; God alone Beholds the end of what is sown;

Beyond our vision short and dim The harvest-time is hid with Him.

In manus Tuas commendo spiritum, animam, corpus meum; creasti, redemisti, et regenerasti illa,

Domine, Deus Veritatis.

4.

But, unforgotten though it lies,

That seed of generous sacrifice,

Though seeming on the desert cast, Shall rise with bloom and fruit at lash

Propter Nomen tuum, Domine, vivificabis me; injustitia tua educes de tribulatione animam meam.

Mane nobiscum, Domine, quoniam advesperascit,

Et inclinata est jam dies laboriosæ hujus vitæ.

Amen! Amen! Amen!

• •

◯∴ Lo! THAT WHICH WAS THE ARCHITECT!

⊕∴ The place where the one murdered was hidden.

....

☉∴ O Lord, my God! Was there no help for the Widow's Son! The Master's word is lost!

....

☉∴ Venerable Brethren, the Master Khurum is dead. So must Death shortly overtake us all If it comes to any of us as suddenly and unexpectedly, may it find us as well prepared, in the strength of virtue and good deeds. He died rather than betray his trust.

....

Venerable Brother Azariah, you will take order for conveying these venerated remains to the Temple: and the Most Venerable Brother Adonai-ram will cause a sarcophagus to be carved, to receive it, after the manner of the Egyptians, and a grave to be prepared near the Temple, over which shall be set a tomb of marble, seven cubits in length, five in height, and three in breadth. Also the letters upon this Seal shall be engraven on a triangular plate of gold, and that be set firmly in one face of a cube of agate, and the whole deposited in a place known to the Masters, that the Word may by study, reflection and prayer be in due time recovered.

....

☉∴ Know, thou who hast represented the Master Khurum, living and dead that so he died, and so his remains were discovered and disposed of. That the legend was a symbol, was indicated by the ceremonial that followed.

••

הנדרים.

Renewal………Secrecy.

••

To the Glory of the Grand Architect of the Universe, in the name and under the auspices, etc., and by virtue of the powers vested in me as Master of this Worshipful Lodge of Master Masons,………….and I do endow you, as a most precious treasure, with the title of Venerable Brother, which you should always endeavor to deserve and worthily wear.

••

⊙∴ As a Master Mason, you will wear the apron with the flap turned down. Its material and color signify purity and innocence: and its bordering of blue, which is the color of Venus, loving-kindness or charity.

••

⊙∴ Receive again your Sword. Once it was the weapon of a Knight and Gentleman. As the symbol of Loyalty and Honor, it is the fit weapon of a Master Mason.

••

☉∴ As a Master Mason, you will sit covered in the Lodge. So the Commons of England sit, being the representatives of a free people. This custom is older than the English Commonwealth, having always prevailed among Masons. Hitherto you have served, as an Apprentice and Fellow-craft. As a Master, you are to command and direct. See that you do not abuse your powers!

••

FINAL INSTRUCTION.

••

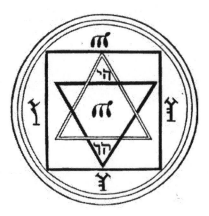

••

Once more we lead you back to the ancient Mysteries: "The ceremony of Initiation," says the Chief Priest to Lucius, in Apuleius, "into the Mysteries, is, as it were, to suffer death, with the precarious chance of resuscitation."

The Goddess, he said, selected only such persons as might through her Providence be in a manner born again, and commence the career of a new existence.

All initiation is but introductory to the great change of Death. Everything earthly must die. Man, like Œdipus, is wounded from his birth: his real Elysium can exist only beyond the grave. Death is the inseparable antecedent of life: the seed dies, in order to produce the plant; the worm dies to produce the brilliant moth. The death of the seed in giving birth to the plant, connecting the sublimest hopes with the plainest occurrences, was the simple, yet beautiful formula assumed by the great Mystery in almost all religions, from the Zend-Avesta to the Gospel.

The Hierophants of Samothrace assured those initiated into their Mysteries, of the rewards reserved for the virtuous after death, by the justice of the Gods. In the Mysteries of Eleusis, the

Initiate was taught that the Soul was the whole of man; that earth was but his place of exile ; that Heaven was his native country; that for the Soul to be bora is really to die ; and that death was for it the return to a new life.

••

Life is a school for the Soul, an arena in which, amid calamity, suffering and evil, it may learn to practice the manly and heroic virtues. It is fitted by the Divine Wisdom for a place of instruction and discipline. Can any better means of instructing, disciplining and invigorating the Soul be imagined, than are afforded by the trials and sufferings, the reverses and disappointments, the triumphs and defeats, the satisfactions and mortifications of this life?

Everywhere, and in all their forms, the Mysteries were funereal, and celebrated the mystical death and restoration to life of some divine or heroic personage; and the details of the legend, and the modes of the death varied in the different countries where the Mysteries were practiced.

Everywhere, also, this mythical personage primarily symbolized the Sun, which, descending southward in Autumn until he reached the Tropic of Capricorn at the Winter Solstice, was then said to die and be buried, for the few days that he seemed undetermined whether to continue to tend further and further southward, until he should leave the world in perpetual night; or to begin again to ascend toward the Equator; and this ascent, after the Solstice, was called his resurrection, aphanism or regeneration .

Everywhere, also, the personage of the legend was a beneficent being or Deity, the personification of Light; a Hero, an Intercessor and Mediator for men, a Saviour and Redeemer.

••

The fruit of the sufferings of the God, Father of Light and Souls, slain by the Chief of the Powers of Darkness, and again restored to life, was acquired in the Mysteries. 'His death works your salvation! ' said the High Priest of Mithra. That was the great secret of this religious tragedy, and its expected fruit; the resurrection of a God, who, re- possessing himself of his dominion over darkness, should associate with him in his triumph those virtuous Souls that by their purity were worthy to share his glory: those that did not strive against the divine force that drew them to him, when he had thus conquered.

Life rising out of death was the great Mystery, which symbolism delighted to represent under a thousand ingenious forms. Nature was ransacked for attestations to the grand Truth which seems to transcend all other gifts of imagination, or rather to be their essence and consummation. Such evidences were easily discovered. They were found in the olive and lotus, in the evergreen myrtle, in the deadly but self-renewing serpent, the wonderful and brilliant moth emerging from the coffin of the worm, the Phoenix born of its own ashes, the scarabæus, the phenomena of germination, the settings and risings of the Sun and Stars, the darkening and growth of the Moon; and Sleep, the minor mystery of death. The typical death of the Nature-God was a profound and consolatory mystery. The origin of the doctrine of the Soul's immortality is as remote and untraceable as the origin of man himself.

● ●

That name, ordinarily rendered Hiram, is in the book of Kings, Khairom or Khairom, but in that of Chronicles Khurom or Khurum. It was either exclusively Phoenician (or Tsurian), or both Hebrew and Phoenician; for that of the King of Tsur was the same. אדנירם, Adonairam, was also a Tsurian name.

In 2 Chron, ii. 13, the King of Tsur writes to Solomon; "I send thee a skillful workman, חורם אדי, Khurum Abai;" which our translation renders 'of Huram my father's.' Ab-i is 'my father.' In 2 Chron, iv. 16, we find חורם אבין, Khurum Abiu, which means, and is rendered by, 'Huram his father:' The last word, Abiu, has been transformed into Abiff, and become part of the name, which it is not. Ab, in the Hebrew, meant not only father, ancestor, progenitor, but also Master. For the meaning of the name of the Master, we refer you to the Morals and Dogma of the Kite.

● ●

It has sometimes happened that a free people has lost its freedom, conquered by foreign arms. Sometimes liberty has been sold. But when a Free State has ceased to be free, it has generally been because its people have unwittingly connived with a Tyrant or Usurper. It is true that those who, in a free Commonwealth, under the stale pretences of necessity, and the safety of the People, by virtue of their Magistracy or military rank, usurp the powers of Dictator, and barbarously violate the most sacred rights of their Country, deserve the names of rebels and traitors, not only against the laws of that Country, but against Heaven itself. But it is equally true that wherever an inveterate resolution has been formed to annihilate the liberties of the governed, it is in the power of the people to prevent it, and that history affords examples of successful resistance by force to usurpation by arms.
● ●

Seek out the great and wise men, and intrust the fortunes of the Republic, as far as your vote and influence can do so, to their hands. Select those for office, who will more add honor to the office, than the office will honor them; those who are entitled by their intellect and learning to deal on equal terms with the Republic, and to lay her under obligations by accepting her offices.

The Country that has no such men, is indeed a pauper. The State that has them and does not use their services, is idiotic or insane.

••

Be always jealous of power, which ever tends to perpetuate itself and to increase. Usurpations generate like vermin. The men of energy are always for burning the parchment. Never listen to those who cry that your free government is too weak and inefficient; and who urge you to give it the power to take the last shilling from your purse, the last drop of blood from your veins. Give this power to no man or set of men, however worthy he or they may seem of such trust. If a people part with it, they resign their liberties. Even in struggling to attain its independence, a Nation may lose its freedom. A people true to itself needs no Saviour, to achieve its political salvation. If it so wills, it is sufficient for itself.

And, whatever follies or excesses a Republic, its rulers or its people may commit, let not these alienate you from a free form of government, and enlist you under the banners of despotism, even in opinion. No government is free from imperfections and evils; and we are always sure to imagine that those under which we suffer are the least tolerable of all. The election of unfit and incapable persons, in many instances, is inseparable from republican governments. But petty and base men not only attain power under Kings, but become Kings themselves; and the truly wise and great as rarely govern in Monarchies as in Democracies. It is human nature that is in fault. As yet, free government is an experiment. After a time, it will succeed. It is the only form of government that consists with individual rights and the dignity of human nature: and if it be impossible for a Community of freemen wisely to govern itself, it is absurd for man to claim to have been made a little lower than the Angels, and in the image of God.

••

Some of the emblems usually exhibited in the Master's degree are ancient and some modern. The bee-hive, for example, is modern. The trite explanation given of it does not even merit a passing word. The adherents of the Stuarts, in England and on the Continent, after Charles the First was executed, resorted to Masonry as a means of organization and communication. The Pretender's Son, as he was after- wards popularly called, still exercised high Masonic powers, as the lineal inheritor of Masonic Sovereignty: and there is still extant a brief of Constitution of a Chapter of Rose- Croix of Heredom at Arras in France, granted by him, the unfortunate Charles Edward Stuart. Before the Restoration, the Loyalists were especially active through their secret organization; and the Masonic legend was used by them as a parable or allegory, the interpretation of which was the execution of Charles, brought about by a rebel Parliament and army, and Scottish Presbyterian treachery. Since then, English Masonry has always inculcated submission and obedience to the powers of the State, whatever they might be. Thus denaturalized, it adopted the bee-hive as one of its emblems; because it represented a Commonwealth or people governed by a King, or the Constitution of the British Government.

This is the key to those 'Ancient Charges and Regulations,' by which every Master elect of an English Lodge promises 'to be a peaceable subject, and not to be concerned in plots and conspiracies against Government; but patiently to submit to the decisions of the Supreme Legislature.'

■ ■

The forty-seventh problem of Euclid, the only explanation whereof, given in the English Rite, is, that 'it teaches Ma- sons to be general lovers of the Arts and Sciences,' is in reality one of those Etruscan Stones, as it were, built into the whimsically incongruous walls of that system of Masonry. It is the profoundest philosophical symbol of the whole science. Like a boulder of granite in a great alluvial plain, brought thither at some remote and unknown period, from the far-distant mountains, by some cataclysm or iceberg from Northern glaciers, when that which is now dry land was covered by the waters of a deep sea, it stands unexplained, a Sphynx, its meaning not even guessed at by those who have denaturalized and trivialized the Symbols of Masonry. The true meaning will be orally told you, at the proper time.

■ ■

The field of study here opened to you is very great. It is because of the Triad in every system of philosophy and religion, and the number seven, composed of four and three, in all the sacred creeds and mystic teachings, from the earliest times to Christianity and Gnosticism that the 47th Problem and the greater and lesser Tetractys were the great symbols of Pythagoras. Even Plutarch, himself an Initiate, has not given us the true key to its meaning.
■ ■
The working-tools of a Master Mason are not given alike, even in the same Rite. Some say they are the Holy Bible, Square and Compasses: others that there is but one, the Trestle-Board: others that they, are all the implements of Masonry indiscriminately, but especially the Trowel. The Hebrews worked in rebuilding the Temple, with the Sword in one hand and the Trowel in the other. The Trowel is the chief working-tool of the Master. It is the cement spread by the Trowel that makes solid the walls, and gives the building permanence. Loving-kindness, mutual con- cession, mutual forbearance, toleration of opinion, may well be termed the cement that binds men together in society. Harmony and concert of action between the Departments, each refraining from usurpation of power, or even stopping short of the line up to which it might push its prerogative, are essential to the perpetuity of the State. Sympathy is the cohesive force

that binds men together, in Orders and Societies; and when it ceases to exist or is weakened, and selfishness usurps upon it, the Order or the State draws nigh unto its end. When self-interest and self-aggrandizement are deified, as the Roman Emperors were in their lives, calamities are at hand.

The accomplished Mason applies to their uses the Symbolic Level, Plumb and Square. He uses also the Compasses and other instruments of Geometry, if invested with power or the authority of the Intellect that others may work by his designs: and if need be, he draws the Sword, as the Soldier of Truth and Justice, and the Defender of the rights of Man.

In a country where every expression of opinion is for- bidden, and independence, the true national life, can only be obtained by revolt, revolt can only be effected by conspiracy. There, Masonry and men must teach, incite, arm and fight by conspiracy. It is the dire necessity imposed on them. They have to earn and win the privilege of de- bate and discussion. They argue with an opponent who smites them on the mouth, and buries them within walls of stone. They must talk in whispers, assemble in the night, and deal their blows in the shape of insurrection and revolt. Even to hiss and sting is sometimes Nature's great conservatism. The god Vishnu, trodden near to death by a huge elephant, transforms himself to a snake that he may again appear as a divine man. To have mind and speech and free discussion, so that the Citizen and the Priest may meet each other face to face, and each hear what the other has to say, Reason sitting as arbiter and judge, the Soldier must be made to stand aside, and let the Thinker argue with the Priest. If you live in a country where the truth may safely and openly be spoken, so much the more imperative a duty it is for you to speak it. The whole world is the field of that husbandry. Everywhere the good seed may be sown; and with God's blessing it may everywhere yield as bountifully as the yellow grain.

Learn, my Brother, that the great lesson which Masonry teaches is, to think better of the world in which we live, and especially of our Brethren; and so to value the one as to think it worthwhile to try and make it nobler and better, and the others, as to be never willing to have the bonds of Brotherhood broken.

None cheat themselves more than those who fail to learn all there is about them which tends to lift us up above the low cares of life. To know what has been that is great and noble among the scenes around us is to furnish the world within our view in a way that art cannot vie with. No wealth can give the joy that we feel when we fill our minds with a sense of the fact that we live and breathe and act on the spots or around the scenes where great men have moved and acted.

We owe it to our country to kindle the patriotism of our people by giving proof of the reverence in which we hold the memories of all who have made sacrifices for its welfare. The duty of honoring our fathers is not only enjoined as one of a religious character or as a bond which strengthens family ties, but it is also one which upholds and strengthens States.

We are equally bound not unjustly to depreciate the living, lest in doing so we rob the Country of honor to which these entitle her.

Thank Heaven, much as there may be in this life and in its rivalries and jealousies to make us uncharitable, there are recognized truths enough, with which to build up a glorious world, if men would but build. That is now your duty. 'It is happier to love than to hate. Temperance is the line which divides pain from pleasure.' There is a whole system of morals in these truisms. If that which no one denies as moral truth had but its legitimate sequence in human action, the world would be revolutionized. There is regen- oration for mankind in the simple words Justice and Temperance. Industry, Activity and Energy are but our very life itself; the putting forth of the power that is within us. If men were active to good ends, temperate, just and equitable, the earth would be peopled with prosperous and contented multitudes.

Money can buy many things, good and evil; but all the wealth of the world cannot buy one friend, and could not pay us for the loss of one. We are but poor and improvident spendthrifts, if we let one friend drop off through inattention, or let one thrust another aside, or if we hold aloof from one for petty jealousy or heedless slight, or roughness. Would you throw a diamond away, because it pricked you? One good friend, one true Masonic Brother, is not to be weighed against the jewels of all the earth. Will you lose one, because he is once or twice or ten times unkind or unjust to you? Will you not let him excuse himself? Will you not remember your own failings and forgive him? If there come coolness or unkindness between you, come face to face, and have it out, and that quickly, before love grows cold. Life is too short to quarrel in, or to carry black thoughts of friend or Brother. Say always, "If I was wrong, I am sorry: if you were, then I am sorrier yet, for surely I should grieve for my friend's or Brother's misfortune. And the mending of your fate does not lie with me, but the forgiving it does, and that is the happier office." Clasp hands, and let the Past be: and thank Heaven that you still keep your friend or Brother. For either is too precious a thing to be lightly held; and a new one will not come for calling, nor make up for an old one, when he comes.

Finally, learn not to dread death. You propose to yourself many pleasures and much content, in the years that are to come. If it is death to part with these delights, surely the mind can conceive others afterward. And one who truly puts his trust in our Father who is in Heaven, and does not merely say so without his heart answering cordially to the words, and who believes that there is an- other and a better life after this, ought to be content (after a pang or two of separation from dear friends here), to put his hand into that of the summoning Angel, and say, 'Lead on, O Messenger of God, our Father, to the next place whither the Divine Goodness calls us.' We must be blindfolded, before we can pass, we know: but we should have no fear about what is to come, any more than our children need fear that the love of their father will fail them.

Live as a Mason should, that you may die as a Mason should. To meet with all men upon the Level, to act with them according to the Plumb, and to part with them upon the Square, are the requisitions of the law of Masonry. May you always so meet, act and part, and may your labors not fail of their reward!

♫

CONGRATULATION ON THE ADVANCEMENT OF THE BROTHER.

••

The Catechism is repeated, if there be time. Generally it will be postponed to another meeting.

••

TO CLOSE.

••

APPENDIX.

OFFICES OF CONSECRATION

OF

A HALL OF FREE-MASONS

OF

The Ancient and Accepted Scottish Rite.

OFFICES OF CONSECRATION.

PRELIMINARY DIRECTIONS.

A Hall of Free-Masons of the Ancient and Accepted Scottish Rite in the Southern Jurisdiction of the United States will be consecrated (i. e., dedicated or devoted) to the uses and purposes of the Bite, by the single Body or all the Bodies jointly, that are to labor in it; the single Body or the lowest, if there be more than one, being first regularly opened, and the officers in their proper stations and places. If there he more than one, the principal officers of all will sit together, each in his proper station or place; those of the highest on the right, and all properly clothed.

In the North will be three lights; in the South, five ; in the West, seven; and in the East, nine ; as in a Lodge of Perfection; and on the South, West, and East sides of the Altar nine large lights, three on each of these sides, arranged in triangles, the apex of each toward the Altar.

The hangings should be of crimson.

On the altar of obligation, the English Bible, Hebrew Pentateuch , and Book of Constitutions, and on these two swords crossed, and upon them the Tau Cross.

The altar of incense will be in the north; and in front of the station of each of the three principal officers a small table. On that in front of the third officer will be a silver vessel containing oil of olives; on that in front of the second, a vessel of glass, containing red wine; and on that in front of the first, and a gilded vessel containing grains of wheat. In front of the orator will be a table, and upon it, in a vessel of glass, pure water.

The offices will be performed by an Inspector General or Deputy of the Supreme Council, if one be present, or by the Presiding Officer of the single or highest body.

When the dignitaries, officers, and members of the Body or Bodies have taken their places, the Lights in the four quarters of the Hall, and those at the Altar will be extinguished; and thereupon the offices will commence.

The Committee charged with the preparation and furnishing of the Hall will apply for admission, be announced and enter, and advance to the altar of obligation, when the Chairman will report to the Presiding Officer in the East. He may do so in the following or other appropriate words:

THE CHAIRMAN.

M∴ Puissant Grand Master (M... Wise Master, or other proper title): The Committee of Mithras Lodge of Perfection (or other Body or Bodies, as the case may be), intrusted with the charge of preparing, furnishing, and decorating this Hall for the uses and purposes of the Ancient and Accepted Scottish Rite of Free-masonry in the degrees here to be worked, has endeavored faithfully to perform the duty so imposed upon it; and doth now, by me, its Chairman, ask that its work may be inspected, and if found to be well done, be accepted by the Lodge, and the Committee discharged.

M M∴ My Brethren, you have heard the report of your Committee, and you see their work. If it is acceptable to you, and you are content therewith, empower me to say so and to thank your Committee, by the affirmative sign.

If the Brethren do thus signify their approval, the Presiding Officer will say:

M∴ Brother Chairman and Brethren of the Committee: The Brethren find your work acceptable and are content with it; and do by me now return you their thanks, the welcome wages of a true and zealous Mason; and having well and faithfully performed its duty, the Committee is discharged. You will please be seated among the Brethren.

MUSIC.

After which, the Master rising, will rap once, and say:

M∴ My Brethren, this Hall is now prepared for the uses of the Bodies of the Ancient and Accepted Scottish Rite that are here to labor for the advancement of the Order and the good and happiness of each other; here to listen to and teach the lessons of morality and wisdom contained in our Rituals ; here to learn and practice Charity and Toleration ; here to learn to know each other better and love each other more; and here to entitle themselves to the thanks and gratitude of the widow and the orphan, and of distressed and destitute Brethren. Is it your pleasure that this Hall shall now be consecrated, dedicated, and devoted to these and the other great and holy purposes of the Scottish Free-masonry? If so, give me the affirmative sign.

This being given, the Master will say, addressing the Inspector General or other Officer, who is to act as Consecrator:

M∴ Illustrious Sovereign, Grand Inspector General, the Brethren of Mithras Lodge of Perfection (and other Bodies, if any there be,) desire that this Hall, in which they are here- after to assemble and work, shall now be consecrated to the purposes of the Scottish Free-masonry, to that noblest of all human work and discipline, the acquisition of wisdom, and the increase of loving-kindness and beneficence. Here we intend all to walk in one way and inhabit that one house of the Ancient and Accepted Scottish Bite, in which we are all dwellers; here to press onward with whatsoever of Faith, Hope, and Charity has been our present succor, from that whereunto we have already attained, that we may enter further into the same great reality— not outwardly, or in form and profession only, but in the spirit and the truth, making the teachings of our Ritual our one common rule and guide of all our daily lives.

Here we desire to show in our little circle what unity and affection there are between the most distant members of our Masonic Commonwealth; how the Brethren of the Ancient and Accepted Scottish Rite, living in many lands and speaking many tongues, make up one family, their participation in one communion of doctrine and purpose rendering them a single body throughout the world; that here may be discerned the true supply of that want of our nature, which craves fellowship and sympathy, the warnings of kindness when our feet slip in dangerous places, consolation and encouragement in ill-fortune and adversity.

You have been pleased to consent to perform these Offices of Consecration. Permit me to place in your hand the gavel of direction, and to surrender to you this station. [He raps three, the Brethren all rise and salute, and the Inspector General or other Consecrator, proceeds to the East, accepts the gavel, seats the Brethren with one rap, and takes his seat.]

Then the Choir chaunts as follows:

CHAUNT.
In Domino Confido.

In the Lord put | I my | trust: how say ye then to my soul that she should flee as a | bird un | to the | hill?

The Lord is in His | holy | Temple: the Lord's seat | is in | Heaven.

His eyes con | sider the | poor: and His eyelids | try the | children of | men.

For the righteous Lord | loveth | righteousness: His countenance will behold the | thing j that is | just.

O send out Thy Light and Thy Truth, that | they may | lead me: and bring me unto Thy holy | hill, and | to Thy | dwelling.

O sing unto God and sing praises | unto His | Name:

Magnify Him that rideth upon the heavens as it were upon an horse; praise Him in His name Yah, | and re | joice be l fore Him.

Prais-ed be God who hath not cast | out our | prayer: nor | turned His | mercy | from us.

Then the Consecrator, rising, says:

C∴ My Brethren, those who consecrate to the laudable uses and good purposes of Free-masonry that which is to be an Holy House of the Temple, should do so with earnestness and gravity, not unmindful during the solemn ceremonies of the renewed pledges that they do thereby give, and new promises, which not to keep faithfully involves falsehood and dishonor. Even as we renew the pledge of brotherhood whenever we address or speak of another as our Brother, so when we call the place in which we assemble a Sanctuary or a Temple, we renew our pledge that we will by our conduct and conversation, in our daily lives, make it to be what we call it

You propose now to consecrate this Hall, by solemn and symbolic ceremonies, to the uses and purposes of the Ancient and Accepted Scottish Bite. I need not repeat to you what those are, in detail. No one who devotes himself to them can ever have cause to regret it; for its lessons, if well learned and practiced, will enable him to bear adversity without impatience, and prosperity without arrogance or vanity. Cherishing loving-kindness for his fellows, judging charitably their actions, and censuring no one's opinions, he may enjoy the inestimable blessings of the warm, cordial, and perpetual sympathies of a genuine brotherhood.

Surrounded by your symbols, sanctified by an immense antiquity, you learn from them the lessons of a wise religious philosophy older than history, and which Pythagoras learned from those whose ancestors knew them in the days of the Bactrian Zarathustra.

To make your Order the great benefactor of humanity, nothing is needed except that its children shall prove equal to the mission undertaken by them, true to their obligations and worthy of their titles, which also are pledges for faithful performance of duty. The foundations have been well laid; the beginnings have been glorious; it needs now only that those shall not be wanting who must complete the structure. There will be found those who can rightly counsel, exhort, and inspire; and if men are not wanting for the execution, are not unworthy because lukewarm and indifferent, the Order will neither die nor decay, but reap a rich harvest of the truest glory—the glory of good deeds and benefits.

These results, to which we all can contribute, may not come during our little day of life. But every one of us may make the teachings of our Rituals to be of inestimable benefit to himself. We may make it a habit for ourselves to think charitably, speak kindly, and act justly, holding that the greatest possible evil which can happen to a man is his own injustice, and that the crime of him who retaliates is greater than that of him who first injures; that peace, moderation, content, justice, and virtue constitute the happiness of a man, and that to think well of our fellows, love them notwithstanding their errors, and forgive them when they wrong us, more conduce to one's well-being than to condemn or overcome or punish them.

If it is your intention thus to make this Hall a Holy House of the Temple, let us proceed to consecrate it.

When the Consecrator has ended, the Choir sings the following:

ODE.

Thy Temple stands, O God of grace,

Above our thought, beneath our tread;

Its ample floor, unmeasured space;

Its arch with suns unnumbered spread.

Yet though not space that hath no bound Thy power contains, Thy glory tells;

Upon this little sphere are found Fair places where thy Spirit dwells.

The ancient symbols of Thy truth

Surround us here and speak Thy thought,

Which, when the world was in its youth,

The Sages of the Orient taught.

Here let Thy Wisdom and thy Word Speak in us and be understood;

Nor here be other accents heard Than those of perfect brotherhood.

When the Ode has been sung, the Consecrator will say:

C∴ Brother Orator, as water was brought from the sea-side into the Temple, and poured out there, in the ancient Mysteries of Adonis in Syria; and as in Egypt waters were brought from Lake Meroe to sprinkle in the Fane of Isis, so every morning during the eight days of the Feast of Tabernacles, the Hebrew Priests drew three logs of water, in a golden vessel, from the Fountain of Siloe, and carrying this with great and joyful solemnity, through the water-gate, into the Temple, they poured it out to the southwest of the altar, as a symbol, some of the Talmudists say, of the effusion of the Holy Spirit. Water has in all ages been the natural symbol of purification, and those of the Jordan were deemed holy, as our Aryan ancestors extolled and deified the rivers Sarasvati and Ardvicura. Perform, then, the ancient ceremony of aspersion.

The Consecrator calls up the Brethren.

The Orator takes the vessel of water, goes to the altar, and standing near it, says:

Or∴ As a symbol of purification, and as a pledge of the purity of heart and purpose of the Brethren who are here to work in harmony and loving-kindness, I sprinkle this pure water about the altar of obligation. May our Father who is in Heaven, manifesting His Divine wisdom here, in spire in us wise counsels and make us fruitful of good works and our undertakings prosperous! Amen!

The Orator returns to his place, the Brethren are seated, and the Choir sing the following:

CHAUNT.
Jubilate Deo.

O be joyful in the Lord, | all ye lands: serve the Lord with gladness, and come before His | presence | with a | song.

Be ye sure that the Lord | He is | God: it is He that has made us, and not we ourselves; we are His people, | and the | sheep of His | pasture.

O go your way into His gates with thanksgiving, and into His | Courts with | praise: be thankful unto Him, and | speak good | of His | Name.

For the Lord is gracious, His mercy is | ever | lasting: and His truth endureth from gene | ration to gene | ration

---

Then the Third Officer, standing in his place in the West, the Brethren being called up, will take the vessel of oil, and say:

J∴ W∴ In the name of our Father who is in Heaven,

I consecrate this Hall [here sprinkling the floor with the oil] to Charitable Judgment, Union, and Toleration! May the Brethren who come together here always work in harmony, with indulgence and generosity towards each other; and may they ever pour oil upon the troubled waters of strife and persuade men to be no more censorious or unforgiving! Amen!

Whereupon the Master of Ceremonies will light the three lights on the South side of the Altar, while the Choir sings the following

CHAUNT.

Show us Thy | mercy, O | Lord: and | grant us | Thy salvation.

I will hearken what the Lord God will | say con | cerning me: for He shall speak peace unto His people and to His Saints, that | they turn | not a | gain.

For His salvation is nigh | them that | fear Him: that glory may | dwell | in our | land.

Mercy and truth are | met to | gather: righteousness and | peace have | kissed each | other.

Truth shall flourish | out of the | Earth: and righteousness hath | looked | down from | Heaven.

Tea, the Lord shall show | loving - kindness: and our | land shall | give her | increase.

Righteousness shall | go be | fore Him: and He shall direct His | going | in the | way.

In the Lord put | I my | trust: how say ye then to my soul, that she should flee as a | bird un | to the | hill?

Then the Second Officer, standing in his place in the West, will take the vessel of wine, and say:

S∴ W∴ In the name of the Great Order of Free-Masonry, I consecrate this Hall [here sprinkling with the wine] to Sympathy, Compassion, and Beneficence! May the Brethren who assemble here ever labor to relieve the needy, con- sole the bereaved, and cheer with the wine of contentment the disconsolate! Amen!

Whereupon the Master of Ceremonies will light the three lights on the West side of the Altar.

CHAUNT.
Laudate Dominum.

O praise the Lord, for it is a good thing to sing praises | unto | our God : yea, a joyful and pleasant thing it | is | to be | thankful.

He healeth those that are | broken in | heart : and giveth | medicine to | heal their | sickness.

He helpeth them to right that | suffer | wrong : He | feed | eth the | hungry.

The Lord helpeth them | that are | fallen : the Lord | careth | for the | righteous.

The Lord careth for the strangers; He defendeth the fatherless | and | widow : as for the way of the ungodly, He | turneth it | upside | down.

O praise the Lord, | all ye | heathen : praise | Him, | all ye | nations.

For His merciful kindness is ever more and | more | tow'rds us : and the truth of the Lord endureth forever. Praise | - - | - the | Lord.

Then the Master or other Presiding Officer on the Consecrator's right, standing in his place, takes the vessel of wheat, and says:

M∴ In the name of the Ancient and Accepted Scottish Rite of Free-masonry, I consecrate this Hall [sprinkling with the wheat] to Justice, Right, and Truth! May the Brethren who assemble here ever be true and loyal to these three, which the three stars in the belt of Orion, called of old the Three Kings, in which, since the human race began, no man hath seen even the shadow of change, do represent to us! May they ever labor without wearying in the cause of each! And may every good seed that shall be sown here germinate like the wheat, and in due season bear good fruit!

Whereupon the Master of Ceremonies lights the three lights on the East side of the Altar.

CHAUNT.
Confitemini Domino.

O give thanks unto the Lord, for | He is | gracious : and His | mercy en | dureth for | ever.

Remember us, O Lord! according to the favour that Thou hearest | unto thy | children : O visit | us with | Thy sal | vation.

That we may live, in peacefulness | with each | other : and strive to do good works among men, and give | thanks and | glory | to Thee.

For Thy mercy is greater | than the | heavens : and Thy glory a | bove | all the | Earth.

We will sing of the Lord, because He hath dealt so | lovingly | with us : yea, we will praise the | Name of the | Lord most | Highest.

O let Thy children rejoice | and be | glad : for Thou shalt judge the folk righteously, and be the com | fort- er | of those who | mourn.

When this is sung, the Consecrator says:

C∴ Let now this Hall be lighted by those numbers that had a mysterious and profound significance for the ancient sages of our race, when, upon the summits of the Bactrian mountains, thousands of years ago, they lighted their fires before day, after Mithra, the Morning-Star, had risen, and when below it glittered the three bright stars of Orion, and they waited for the dawn and the sunrise, to begin their sacrifices to the God whose outflowing they deemed the Light to be.

The three, five, seven, and nine lights are now lighted in succession, and the incense is then lighted upon the altar of incense, and the Consecrator or a proper Brother offers up this

PRAYER.

Our Father who art in Heaven! Permit us here to become better, truer, and nobler, and to be of use to men. May the intellectual darkness of Error and Ignorance disappear in Thine own good time before the Light of Knowledge! May the gloomy shadows of envy, ambition, jealousy, faction, ill-will, and discontent be banished hence, and this Hall be ever the abode of Light, which is Thy revelation! May the Great Lights, which Tyrants, temporal and spiritual, dread, shine among the nations! May Faith, Hope, Charity, and Toleration ever enlighten the souls of all who to work come hither; and may Truth, like the sunlight, shine into the darkest souls of nations and of men. If the doctrines that we teach are true, commend them unto men. If they are false, let them not harm mankind nor be mischievous to ourselves; and unto Thee be the Kingdom, the Power, and the Glory, for ever and ever! Amen!

After the prayer the Choir sings the following:

SONG.

The good seed sown with open hand, Is never sown in vain:

Our Father who in Heaven is,

Gives sunshine, dew and rain, Until the ripening Autumn brings The sheaves of golden grain:

Thus bread upon the waters cast Comes unto us again.

Sow on! the hours are fleeting fast,

The seed must drop to-day;

What though the time come not to reap, Before you pass away?

What though your tears rain on the seed?

They'll stir its quiet sleep,

More quickly will the green blades rise For every tear you weep.

We hear the reapers singing, who Into God's harvest go;

Who at the gates of night, whom they Invite, will grope below?

Sow on! and thus climb surely up To where the light appears;

Where you shall reap in gladness what You sow to-day in tears.

No Mason true can walk in vain Life's pleasant shaded ways,

Not helping those who fainting toil,

Or count the workless days:

For "Soul that gives is Soul that lives;"

To bear another's load Makes light one's own, makes short the way, Makes bright the homeward road.

Then the Consecrator says:

C∴ I do declare this Hall duly consecrated, and fit for the good purposes and worthy ends of the Scottish Free- masonry, and pronounce it sacred to the cultivation of all the Masonic virtues, and especially devoted to the diffusion of the great doctrine of Liberty secured by constitutional Law; of Equality of rights, maintained by public Order; of Fraternity, with due and lawful Subordination; to the protection and relief of the widow and the fatherless, and to the improvement and progress of Humanity.

May we, like Abraham and his children, neither vex the stranger nor oppress him! Here may the weary find rest, and the persecuted protection! Here may the wayfarer find food, the head that is houseless and homeless a shelter! so that when it comes to us to die, it may be truly said of us, that we did good in our day and generation, that our titles were not unworthily worn, and our badges not merely un- meaning ornaments. May the beneficence and charity of our fraternity here fall like soft rains upon parched places, gladdening the afflicted as the dews gladden the green leaves and give new life to the thirsting flowers.

And may we all so live, and so perform all the duties that God imposes upon us here, that when we lie down to our last sleep in the narrow grave, His angels may crown our souls with sweet flowers freshly gathered from the lawns of Paradise.

Truth is omnipotent and eternal. Ear from this Hall be ever all guile and deceit, all pretence and hypocrisy! May these never intrude within its doors; but there let stand as constant tilers, Sincerity and Frankness, Earnestness and Plain-dealing, to prevent the approach of any unclean visitor.

In the name of Loving-kindness, which is the spirit and soul of all true religion; in the name of Honor and Duty, inseparable as the Dioscuri; in the name of Truth, which, sown in whatever barren and rocky soil, springs up and yields an hundred fold for use and blessing; in the name of Toleration, to which Masonry erects its altars; in the name of Faith in God and human nature, of Hope, the chief blessing bestowed by Providence on man, and of Charity, divinest of the Virtues, we consecrate this Hall.

May these ceremonies teach us forbearance, inculcate brotherhood, and incite to good offices! May it never come to pass that none shall go forth from the doors of this Hall to visit the sick, the widow and the fatherless, to feed the hungry and clothe the naked, to comfort the desolate, and to protect and succor the oppressed!

While the Brethren continue to assemble here, may this Hall be devoted to great and noble purposes! Within its walls let benevolence and charity be continually inculcated and practiced! Here may the wise and gentle teachings of Masonry bear rich fruit! Here may Masonry labor in the great cause of Justice, Right, and Truth, striving to make men wiser and better, as well as freer, and to diffuse light and true knowledge among the people! Amen!

Join me, my Brethren, in applauding, by the mysterious numbers, the consecration of this Hall.

The battery of the Lodge of Perfection is given in full, with the sign and plaudit.

The Brethren are then seated, and the work proceeds.

Manufactured by Amazon.ca
Bolton, ON